HOME IS NOT HERE

Home Is Not Here

Wang Gungwu

RIDGE BOOKS
SINGAPORE

© 2018 Wang Gungwu

Published under the Ridge Books imprint by:

NUS Press
National University of Singapore
AS3-01-02
3 Arts Link
Singapore 117569

Fax: (65) 6774-0652
E-mail: nusbooks@nus.edu.sg
Website: http://nuspress.nus.edu.sg

ISBN 978-981-4722-92-6 (casebound)

National Library Board, Singapore Cataloguing in Publication Data

Name(s): Wang, Gungwu.
Title: Home is not here / Wang Gungwu.
Description: Singapore: Ridge Books, [2018]
Identifiers: OCN 1027209172 | 978-981-47-2292-6 (casebound)
Subjects: LCSH: Wang, Gungwu--Childhood and youth. | Chinese--Malaysia--
        Malaya--History--20th century--Biography. | Historians--Biography. |
        Scholars--Biography. | Intellectuals--Biography. | China--Study and teaching.
Classification: DDC 950.049510092--dc23

Cover background: Designed by aopsan/Freepik
Designed by: Nur Nelani Jinadasa
Printed by: Markono Print Media Pte Ltd

To my wife Margaret

Our children
Shih-chang (Ming), Lin-chang (Mei), Hui-chang (Lan)

and our grandchildren
Lisheng (Sebastian), Yisheng (Katharine), Kaisheng (Ryan)
and Feisheng (Samantha)

Contents

Why Tell   1

PART ONE · **My Small World**

From Surabaya to Ipoh   19

The World from Green Town   27

A Taste of China   37

Empire's End and Other Spheres   46

My Mother Remembers   51

PART TWO · **Learning to Roam**

War Comes to Malaya   73

Town Boy   78

Another Kind of Learning   86

A New Norm   97

Preparing to Go Home   105

My Mother Remembers the War   111

PART THREE · **To Nanjing**

Extended Family   125

Getting to Nanjing   137

Five Months with My Parents   145

Settling Down to Study   152

My Teachers   160

Learn from Friends   173

My Mother Back in Ipoh   183

PART FOUR · **Ipoh**

Re-orient   193

Starting Over   203

Index   209

Why Tell

SOME YEARS AGO, I started to write the story of growing up in Ipoh for my children. I knew it was also for myself as I tried to remember what my parents were like. My childhood until I was nineteen, with the exception of nine months in 1948, was the only time when I lived with them in the same town. I thought I should tell my children how different my world was before I left home so that they would understand what has changed for them as children and for us as their parents. My wife Margaret knew my story and agreed that I should tell it while I could.

My decision to publish this story came about when I met a group of heritage activists in Singapore. They made me more conscious of the personal dimensions of the past. As someone who has studied history for much of my life, I have found the past fascinating. But it has always been some grand and even intimidating universe that I wanted to unpick and explain to myself and to anyone else who shared my desire to know. Even when I read about the lives of people high and low, I looked from a critical distance in the hope of learning some larger lessons from them. In time, I realized how partial my understanding of the past was. I was using a platform that was dominated by both European historiography and elements of my Confucian self-improvement background.

My heritage friends reminded me that, while we talk grandly of the importance of history, we are insensitive to what people felt and thought who lived through any period of past time. We often resort to literature to try and capture moments of joy and pain, and that can be a help to imagine parts of one's past. But we have too few stories of what people actually experienced. Focusing on local heritage is a beginning. Encouraging people to share their lives might follow. I began to think that what I wrote for my children could be of interest to people who are not family. So I set out to finish my story and have taken it to the time when I left Ipoh in 1949 to study at the newly established University of Malaya in Singapore. My parents moved to Kuala Lumpur after that and never went back to Ipoh. In preparing this account for a wider readership, I have revised and updated parts of the story wherever I could.

—◦◦◦◦◦—

Many friends tell me that they wish they had talked to their parents more when they were alive. I remember thinking the opposite when I was in my teens. I thought that my mother talked too much about China and not enough about the things that I really wanted to know. Instead, I recall how I wished my father would tell me about himself, especially about his life as a child growing up in China along the Yangzi valley. My parents both loved their China very much and, as long as I can remember, they constantly dreamt of returning home.

China was strangely imbalanced in my mind. There was my mother's view of a traditional China that she was afraid would disappear. She wanted her only child to understand something of that. She saw it as her duty to let me know as much as possible because I was growing up in a foreign land.

I thought I should tell the story of how all that came about for my children to read. As I did so, I came to regret I did not talk more with my parents when they were still alive. My mother did finally write about her life and I have included here what I had translated for my children. I wish I had asked her to tell me more. But what I missed most of all was to hear my father talk to me about personal things, about his dreams and what it was like when he was growing up. I sometimes wished that he did not live so close to his ideal of a Confucian father and showed me something of his real self. I would have loved to know how he turned from child to adult in the turbulent times he lived through. Perhaps it is that sense of loss that has driven me to tell this story.

With my mother, Ding Yan, and my father, Wang Fuwen, not too long after our arrival in Ipoh in the mid-1930s.

———◦◇◈◇◦———

Before my mother died in September 1993, she left me with the manu-script of her "memories of fifty years" that she had completed in 1980. She had written it for me in her very neat *xiaokai* 小楷. She said that there were so many things about her life that she wanted me to know, but we had never sat down long enough for her to tell them to me. I read the memoirs with great sadness. There was so much about her life that I had missed by not hearing her tell me face to face. Using parts of her memoirs, I told Margaret and our children about some key moments in her life. When writing my story for our children, I then went on to translate for them to read the relevant parts of what my mother remembered. That would be more authentic. They would have the chance to see her words and thus have a better sense of the mother she was to me. When I decided to publish my growing up story, I thought I should also include her story as annexes to what I have written.

I cannot remember when my mother began to tell me her stories but believe it was even before I started school at the age of five. She did so to make me conscious of my family in China and thus prepare me for our return to China. She wanted to make sure that I would see the total picture of what she knew and therefore would know what to expect. If I had a sister, perhaps my mother might not have told me so much. But as I was an only child and she was far from her home and had no one else to tell her stories to, she made sure I would not forget what she told me. Ours was a first generation nuclear family. Both my parents grew up in extended families that lived under one roof among many close relatives of at least three generations. And other relatives lived nearby, so it was not normally necessary to say much about them.

My mother made sure I absorbed her stories because she told many of them again and again. It was a kind of cultural transmission exercise for her because I never felt that she told her stories for my entertainment. She always exuded a strong sense of duty in everything she did or said, and I soon realized that she was educating me about my identity as the son of my father and someone from families that were deeply rooted in traditional China. She wanted me to know my place in the Wang clan.

She also wanted to do her duty as a Chinese mother to a son born in a distant foreign land.

My mother began with her own story. She was Ding Yan 丁俨, known within her family as 丁佩兰. She was born in the county seat of Dongtai 东台 in Jiangsu province, a coastal town about fifty miles north of the Yangzi River and not far from my father's hometown of Taizhou 泰州. This is a low-lying country close to the saltpans that dotted the coastline, the source of the wealth that her family had enjoyed during the 19th century. The Ding family had come from Zhenjiang 镇江, one of the great cities of the Yangzi delta at the junction of that river and the Grand Canal. Her ancestors included some who had been officials in the Imperial Salt Commission, and some of them continued to be connected with the salt trade after leaving office. Her own branch left Zhenjiang for Dongtai when the Taiping Heavenly Kingdom forces were approaching the city in the middle of the 19th century.

The family, headed by successful literati, expected its young males to concentrate on classical studies as a means to public office. But it also had members who were well connected with the salt business. When the Qing government stopped the imperial civil service examinations in 1904, the Ding males went on studying in the same old way, partly because of family tradition and partly because they did not know what else they could do. But there were some of them who were more practical and turned to business ventures and these branches of the family remained wealthy during the early Republican era.

My mother had an elder brother who followed tradition. She told me how ill prepared he was to make a living in a China that was changing fast. That aroused the practical side of her nature and made her very ambivalent about what young Chinese males should study. With her brother in mind, her view was that, if a boy did not show talent and inclination towards study, he should not be pushed in that direction but should be advised to learn some practical skills. She also had a younger sister who was equally practical. She was very fond of her sister and approved of the way she chose a career as a minor functionary in the local government.

The three Ding children were all born when the family wealth was still intact, when over a hundred members gathered for every meal in a very large house of several courtyards. My mother spoke with awe of the gong that was sounded to call everyone together at meal times. The men ate at their tables in the main hall while she would eat with her mother and sister in the inner hall with all the other women. But this did not last long. Hers was the last generation to partake of this kind of family welfarism. Opium smoking was taking its toll of some of the men, and even some of the women. The end of the Qing dynasty and the disorder that followed, with rival militarists carving up the country, allowed the local garrison soldiers to "tax" the merchants and gentry landlords within their domains at will.

Together with the opium, the warlord exactions finished off the Ding family in Dongtai, although my mother remembers that the main branch of the family in Zhenjiang survived a little longer. Her stories about her family were tinged with regret, but my main impression was how harshly she judged some of the elders of the clan. She harped a lot on the effects of opium, on the waste and extravagance, on the mismanagement of funds, of the bloated size of the extended family and, most of all, on the failure of the males of her family to adapt to rapidly changing conditions in her part of China.

Her family was conventionally and provincially Confucian. The sons were expected to study hard and aim for official careers. Her father had not shown any exceptional ability with his classical studies and was encouraged to help the family manage the salt business. When she was born in 1905, the family was still wealthy but, soon afterwards, its past connections with officialdom were broken after the fall of the Qing dynasty. Thereafter, her father, together with uncles and cousins, struggled to keep the business going and hold the extended family together. It was a losing battle. New kinds of business skills were needed. The family produced nobody with real entrepreneurial talent, nor did they have the connections needed to deal with the unstable republican regime under President Yuan Shikai and his warlord successors. All the Ding family knew was to hang on to their Confucian values and prepare their sons for some kind of book-based career. They might have expected modifications to the imperial traditions that they could have adapted to, but never seem to have doubted that the core of Confucianism would remain the guiding principles of government.

One good thing did happen to my mother after the end of the Manchu rule. She was set to have her feet bound even though the dynasty had fallen and the republican regime supported the radical call to end foot binding for all girls. When she was told that she had to follow the custom, she cried and pleaded with her mother. They both cried but her mother insisted, and the binding continued. The servant who loved her could not bear my mother's cries and pleaded with her mother, pointing to the fact that some families nearby had stopped the barbarous practice. Eventually, her mother relented. I thought my mother's feet were rather small, but she could not say if they might have been bigger had they not been bound at all.

As she grew up, my mother saw her family break up as the business declined. She saw her brother immersed in the Confucian classics all day long, his only pleasure and relaxation being calligraphy and chess. She and her sister were also taught to read and write at home. She was well trained to appreciate prose literature and read widely, including some traditional fiction like the Dream of the Red Chamber that she was not supposed to read. She studied texts about female virtues, all the home duties and various practical arts essential in a large household that she was expected to help her mother manage when she grew up. Her proudest achievement was to cultivate through much practice a beautiful hand in writing the standard *xiaokai* 小楷 calligraphy, a skill all the girls in her family were expected to have. She told me often how hard she had practiced with an older female cousin and how she became as good as her cousin whose calligraphy everyone admired. But she admitted that she could never paint as well as her cousin who was not only the local beauty but also regarded as the most talented woman painter in her town. When I saw her cousin again in Shanghai in 1980, when she was nearly eighty years old, she was still strikingly beautiful and the painted autographed fan she asked me to bring for my mother was a real gem.

I eventually visited Dongtai in April 2010, but I looked in vain for the large house and grounds that my mother talked about. People in the area told me where it had been, and how it had been sold and redeveloped. They pointed out the houses built later on the land, where dozens of families now live. I met members of a family who lived close by who recalled stories of the Ding Gong Guan 丁公馆, the Ding family home.

One of them showed me the bridge over a stream a couple of hundred yards away that is still called Ding Gong Bridge, marking the boundaries of the Ding family lands. While not sure how accurate they were, I was happy that what I saw confirmed my mother's stories.

I was told most of these stories when I was growing up, before the war came to Ipoh in 1941. The first stories were pleasurable. There was no immediate family around us in Ipoh, but they placed our small family of three within a network of numerous aunts and uncles, and cousins near and distant. Further in the background were grandparents and all the kinfolk of their generation. I received meticulous instruction about all the identifiable relatives brought to life by an anecdote or two about each of them, and each was precisely placed in relation to my mother and father and ultimately to me. Thus was my mental world peopled with blood-kin, shadowy on my mother's side except for her brother and sister but, thanks to my mother, sharp and clear about those on my father's side, up to four generations of Wangs.

My mother was always gentler with her stories about my father's family than about her own. Whether this was because she really respected the Wang lineage or thought that her Confucian duty required her to teach me to respect it, I was never sure. It was probably a bit of both, as the Wangs were never wealthy and held firmly to Confucian literati tradition, had no truck with business and stayed clear of opium smoking. At least, that was the positive image she left me with through her carefully selected stories.

—◦⟨⟐⟩◦—

My father, Wang Fuwen 王宓文, also known as Wang Yichu 王艺初, was reticent about himself and did not talk about his family, and I never thought of asking him about his youth. What I know about how he grew up came from my mother, whose curiosity about the Wang clan led her to piece their story together. My father was born in Taizhou in 1903. He was with his parents in Wuchang (now Wuhan) on October 10, 1911, the day the revolution started that ultimately overthrew the Manchu

Qing dynasty. The Wang family, with the help of a Cantonese friend who was doing business in Wuchang at the time, escaped from the city with their lives and returned to Taizhou. My grandfather Wang Haishan 王海山 (Yunchang 允成) had no prospect of government employment. He turned to business and was introduced by friends to work in a bank, but did not seem to have done well in the business world. He later sought other work without much success.

My father had started his education in Taizhou. He greatly admired his granduncle, Wang Zongyan 王宗炎 (Leixia 雷夏), one of the leading Confucian scholars of the time, and studied at the son Wang Yashan's (王冶山) school in Wuchang. There he learnt the classics under the guidance of his uncle who supervised his mastery of the key Confucian classics and encouraged him to write classical prose and taught him to appreciate the best poetry from the Book of Poetry to the great poets of the Tang and Song dynasties. Following his granduncle, my father learned to write in the style of Yan Zhenqing 颜真卿, and then in the ancient *zhuan* style of calligraphy 篆书. He never stopped practicing *zhuan* calligraphy and I recall as a child watching him do that every evening after dinner. In addition, he admired his family's love of the literature of the Six Dynasties, and wrote his own poetry in that style all his life.

By the age of twelve, my father was deemed to have learnt enough of the classics. After he returned to Taizhou, he studied in one of the new modern schools in Taizhou and concentrated on studying English and mathematics, subjects that were completely new to him. When I visited the school with my family in September 2010, I was shown the official history of the school, and found the names of several Wang men who had taught there, including my father for a brief period immediately after he graduated from university in 1925.

After finishing school, my father received a scholarship to study at the Nanjing Higher Normal College, the year when it became the National Southeastern University, the predecessor of the National Central University, the university that my father later determined I should attend. There my father studied Foreign Languages and Education. The university's president was Guo Bingwen 郭炳文, who had been trained in America in the philosophy of education by scholars like John Dewey

A paean to filial piety. My father's *zhuan* calligraphy.

and Paul Monroe of Columbia University. He brought both of them to lecture for several months and made the university famous as the most progressive education centre in the country.

My father spoke with admiration of Guo Bingwen as the man who recruited Tao Xingzhi 陶行知, a fellow alumnus of Columbia University, to head the school of education. Tao Xingzhi, he said, introduced much-needed innovations to educational methods. My father often told me how much he was inspired by what John Dewey, Tao Xingzhi's teacher, had taught a whole generation of teachers in China about the latest ideas in education philosophy. I do not know what my father was like as a young teacher in China and in Malaya, but I do know that he practiced his brand of liberalism when he was the headmaster of Foon Yew High School 宽柔中学 in Johor Bahru in 1959. He is credited with introducing methods of learning and teaching that gained the school its fine reputation, one that it still enjoys today.

For myself, I can say that he was certainly liberal where my education was concerned, allowing me great freedom to enjoy school and read what I wanted. This often worried my mother, who thought I needed more discipline in my life, but my father avoided as much as possible giving me the kind of traditional education that he had to go through. Living far from China, it would have been difficult for him to do otherwise even if he had wanted to, but he practiced what he believed by sending me to an English school where modern teaching methods were gaining ground.

My father chose to study English literature because he felt that he knew enough Chinese literature and needed to improve his understanding of the outside world. He did this knowing that National Southeastern was famous for its scholars of post-Han literature and especially that of the Six Dynasties period, which he loved, and he never lost his fondness of the poetry of that period. When he turned to English literature, he paid special attention to development of its poetry. He was taught by professors who had studied at Harvard, such as Wu Mi 吴宓, a student of Irving Babbit, who introduced the field of comparative literature to China. As a student in the English department, my father remembered fondly a young American professor named Robert Winter, who introduced him to the poetry of Shakespeare, Milton, Pope and the Romantics (notably Wordsworth and Coleridge) and told him about the Chinese influences on Ezra Pound's poetry. All this confirmed the romantic in him, and I believe he was also much influenced by Winter's liberal ideals. Throughout his life he carried in him a conflict between the traditions that he was brought up with and the world of imagination that English literature opened for him.

As I grew up, I began to realize that, although he said little about political matters, my father was at heart deeply patriotic. I think his patriotism came from his university experiences and his admiration for the revolutionary forces in South China that eventually overthrew the warlords that had divided the country and made it so vulnerable to foreign powers. Before the Northern Expedition of the Nationalists captured Nanjing in 1927 and ended a wasted decade, he left the country to teach in the Nanyang. He did teach briefly in Taizhou after graduation and was teaching at Zhongnan High School 锺南中学 in Nanjing when he was encouraged to go to Southeast Asia to teach the children of the Nanyang *huaqiao* (Overseas Chinese).

He keenly supported education for the *huaqiao* and started his new career in Singapore at the Huaqiao High School. There he learnt about the philanthropic work of Tan Kah Kee (Chen Jiageng 陈嘉庚) and the establishment of Xiamen University a few years earlier. He told me later that he began to read the writings of Lim Boon Keng 林文庆, the local Peranakan Chinese intellectual who was president of Xiamen University. He appreciated Lim Boon Keng's ability to marry Western learning with his faith in Confucian precepts, and he greatly admired Lim Boon Keng's translation of the poems in *Li Sao* 离骚, attributed to Qu Yuan 屈原, the famous minister of the state of Chu during the Warring States period. He was amazed at Lim Boon Keng's ability to identify the plants and flowers mentioned in the poems.

My father also taught in Malacca, at Peifeng 培风 High School. The son of one of local community leaders who founded the school, Shen Moyu 沈慕羽, was one of my father's favourite students. Shen Moyu later became an education leader who enthusiastically supported my father's work at Foon Yew High School and played a key role in the development of Chinese schools in post-war and independent Malaysia.

My father was single during his first years in Malaya. But in 1929, he was offered the job of headmaster of the Huaqiao High School, the first Chinese high school in Surabaya, Java in the Netherlands East Indies. He could now afford to get married. He returned to his hometown, Taizhou, to see his parents, and married my mother, the woman they had chosen for him. His father was unemployed and the family was poor. Given their difficulties, the income he could earn outside was important, so he did not stay long after the wedding, and brought his wife with him to Southeast Asia.

The Chinese in Java were different from those in British Malaya in that larger numbers of them were local-born and many more had been resident outside China for generations. Dutch and Indonesian (Javanese) attitudes towards Chinese Peranakan (local-born) and the new immigrants were also very different. In Java, political loyalties were complicated. The Dutch had begun to teach the local-born Chinese to look towards the West, while the new immigrants pressured all those of Chinese descent to be patriotic towards China. At the same time, young Indonesian nationalists were determined that everyone should be loyal towards the new nation that they were about to create, the country to be called Indonesia. Under such conditions, what role was there for the Chinese high schools? It was my father's job to find out.

Both in Surabaya and later in Ipoh, we lived among non-Chinese as well as Hakka, Cantonese, Hokkien and other Chinese who saw us as somewhat strange. Because my father was a teacher, they always treated him with respect, but despite the kindness she encountered, my mother felt that the sooner we returned to China the better, before her son was totally confused as to who he was.

My father shared her concern that we should go home as soon as possible but, when I was growing up, he was curiously optimistic about how much he could teach me about the China that really mattered, the China of classical literature and Confucian thought. He seemed to have thought that, as long as he could provide me with the core of our cultural heritage, there was no fear of being anything but a proper Chinese. He was therefore confident about sending me to a local English school while waiting to return to China. He was an admirer of English literature but had only started to learn the language in his teens. He thought he should give me a chance to learn the language early when I had the opportunity to do so. He seems to have believed that the combination of Chinese and English literary culture would be a good start and fit me better for the modern world. I was aware that my mother was sceptical but bowed to my father's judgment. At the time, they probably thought it would not do any harm because we would return to China before too long.

The Japanese invasion of China wrecked all their plans when I was seven years old. They decided to remain in Ipoh, and did not expect the war to drag on and be followed by the Japanese occupation of Malaya. After the Japanese defeated the British and pushed the war further north in Southeast Asia towards Burma and India, the different communities in Malaya found that their fates could not be more different under Japanese rule. The Japanese used British census categories of Malays, Chinese and Indians to support Japan's divisive policies. They declared that the Malays, as indigenous people, were to be protected against the others. They encouraged Indians to fight for their country's independence from the British Empire with Japanese help. The Chinese they set apart as enemies of Japan or at the very least as unreliable unless they acknowledged the Wang Ching-wei puppet government in Nanjing, which the Japanese controlled. Some Chinese and a few Malays and Indians, together with many Eurasians, continued to hope for Britain's return and secretly supported underground activities, but the main consequence of occupation was to harden suspicion and distrust among the main races in the country.

We survived the war and, with the return of the British to Malaya and of the Nationalists to Nanjing, my parents again prepared to return to China. As we waited to travel back, civil war resumed in North China, but this did not deter my parents. When we finally left for China, our return had been delayed for more than ten years. I entered the National Central University in Nanjing and studied in the Department of Foreign Languages and Literature. My parents told me how hard I would have to work to become a useful person in post-war China. They knew I had become someone different from what they had hoped for. Nevertheless, my father was optimistic that a few years at the university living among Chinese teachers and fellow students would remedy all that. My mother was more hardheaded and wondered what I could be useful for. At best, she hoped that, with my foreign educational background, I could serve the country as a diplomat.

I did not in the end spend the years in China that they thought necessary to make me more Chinese. Turning away from a China that looked to Stalin's Russia and later became violently opposed to China's heritage, I was neither the kind of Chinese this new China wanted, nor the kind that my father hoped I would become in order to be a useful citizen. The China that he loved could not survive the tribulations that Chinese society went through during the past century. My parents had hoped that the Nationalists would win and tried to settle down to a new life in Nanjing, but it was not to be. My father fell dangerously ill that winter. My mother was convinced that he could not survive another winter under the harsh living conditions that his school provided, and insisted on returning to Ipoh. At the end of 1948, nine months after they left for Malaya, the situation was hopeless for the Nanjing government and I abandoned my university studies to join them. Wars of independence were underway in Indonesia and Vietnam, and in 1948 a conflict known as the Emergency broke out when the British determined that they had to take military action against the Malayan communists. That stage of my life was thus linked to war to an unexpected degree, so much so that I almost viewed war as normal.

My Small World

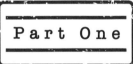

From Surabaya to Ipoh

I WAS BORN in Dutch-ruled Surabaya in 1930 when the Great Depression had brought the capitalist world to its knees. We were far from China, a country divided by warlords and now threatened with invasion by Imperial Japan, the new maritime power. My story really begins with the three of us trying to get back home, to China, but only getting as far as Ipoh, in British Malaya. For the next fifteen years, there were other tries and failures. The three of us did go to Nanjing in 1947. But there was to be no happy return. My parents abandoned the idea after eight months. Nine months later, before the city fell to the communists, I too stopped trying and went back to the town where I had grown up.

Waiting to go to China and returning to Malaya shaped my life more than I realized. Now that I am old, I find so much of my life to be traceable to those two places, and can see that my early story has a double perspective. An image of Nanjing reminds me of what I seemed to be looking for several times in my life while Ipoh represents the world of multiple cultures that I lived with and learnt to love.

Years afterwards, after having moved around in three continents, I understood that calling Ipoh my hometown was not mere sentiment. I spent most of the first nineteen years of my life in different parts of the town. It was a place in the shadow of an imagined ancestral China, but growing up there brought forth an affection for the Malay state under British protection that has stayed with me. Similarly, although I have no close connections with the city, Nanjing left a deep mark in my mind. Recalling the time I spent there, I find myself thinking about other parts of my life and cannot help relating these memories to what I later experienced.

I was a year old when my parents moved from Surabaya so I remember nothing about that city. Two photographs have survived from that year.

One shows me as a baby seated, with a tall Javanese woman standing beside me. My mother told me that the woman fed and bathed me and spoke to me in Malay. The other has me in the arms of the gardener who worked in my father's school. In the photographs, I look well cared for, lucky to be my mother's first and only child.

Me and my Javanese nanny.

My father had been appointed in 1929 to be headmaster of the city's first Chinese high school. Unluckily for him, the Depression spread to Java and the island's sugar industry collapsed. The private school supported by local Chinese businessmen was immediately in financial trouble. After another year of uncertainty, my father resigned. The school could not afford to repatriate us to China, so he settled for a job closer by, in Malaya. One of the school board members gave my father the money to pay our fares to Singapore. There he found a job as assistant inspector of Chinese schools and set off to Ipoh, the state's largest town. In his mind, this was a staging post on the way to China. Little did he know that Malaya would be his and his wife's resting-place and China would become a long shadow for his son.

It was many years later before I realized that my father's experience was one that many Chinese had to face at that time. When I turned from my history research to write about what was changing for his generation, I learnt about the conditions at the beginning of the 20th century and how different those conditions became after the end of the Second World War. I saw that people like my father provided a starting-point for my understanding of what happened, but was also a barrier to understanding those with other backgrounds, not to say those who did not move from China to the Nanyang but migrated to other parts of the world. That reminds me to say that migration studies had not been my primary interest. What drew me to that subject was what China meant to the world outside, especially to those Chinese who had left the country and settled abroad. In addition, I became interested also in what that world knew and thought of China. And they were issues that came initially from my memories of Ipoh and Nanjing.

⎯⎯◁◈▷⎯⎯

The Kinta valley in which Ipoh was the largest town was famous for its tin mines. Nothing connected it to the China that my parents left behind except that it looked like a Chinese town. The Chinese majority in the town owned most of the shops and lived above them. Many of the grand houses were the homes of Chinese mining families. They came mainly from the southern province of Guangdong and were Hakka and Cantonese speakers. Those from Fujian who spoke Hokkien included the local-born from the British colony of Penang.

My parents originated from provinces to their north and understood none of their dialects. Ours was a variety of Mandarin close to the *guoyu* (national language, Mandarin) used for instruction in Chinese schools. People from those parts of coastal China further north who could speak

Mandarin were employed as schoolteachers, and because of that, my father could talk to teachers under his care. The businessmen who ran the school boards somehow managed to understand him. My mother learned some Cantonese so that her servant, Ah Lan, could more or less understand her. Her local Chinese friends, however, could barely comprehend what she tried to say in that dialect and she never managed to speak it properly.

I learnt my Cantonese from Ah Lan and that was my first lesson about China: that there were many kinds of Chinese, and that we were different. It was one reason why my parents did not entertain. The only visitors to our house were a handful of schoolteachers, usually from small towns outside Ipoh, who came to ask my father for advice or help. They were mostly from Jiangsu or Zhejiang provinces and spoke Mandarin with a variety of accents. I would ask my mother who they were and she would tell me how some of them had problems with the state education office, others with their school boards, and yet others brought their personal problems. Many of them lived far out in small mining towns or rubber estates where their primary schools were located. She would then tell me that we, too, were far away from home and, like most of them, we too would not be staying long but would return to China when the opportunity came for us to do so.

Every so often, she would find reason to tell me about my father's long-term plan for us. I was made keenly aware of this when I was five years old and we prepared to visit my grandparents. She explained how she married my father in Taizhou and left for Java shortly after the wedding, and what my father did in Surabaya as a high school principal. She also told me that I was sickly in my early childhood and suffered from asthma, and how little she knew about having a baby and how helpless she was in a foreign land living among people whose languages she could not speak.

My father sent me to an English primary school and I had just started when China arose on the horizon or, perhaps more accurately, it came out of the shadows. I knew that China was our home. The one subject that was a constant was when my parents spoke about family in China and what they could do to make the lives of their close relatives better. They had not been back since they married, and my grandparents had never seen me. I therefore took for granted that there would be a green light to go home and was not surprised when told that it was time for us to do so. What I did not expect was that we were not really going home to live but merely to visit for a few weeks. This was in the middle of 1936. My mother explained that my father was eligible for home leave and had decided to spend it visiting our family. We were not going back to stay because war between China and Japan was imminent and my grandparents had asked my father to keep his good job in Ipoh so that he could continue to send money home when the war began. I accepted that as an example of the filial piety that I already knew was the most important value for all Chinese.

As preparation for my return some day, my mother had begun to teach me simple Chinese characters when I was only three years old. I cannot recall what I actually learnt. She bought a packet of character-cards used for teaching the written language. She told me later that I could remember scores of Chinese characters after a few days and she proudly told my father about what I was able to remember. After a while, my father the modern educationist became concerned that she was pushing me too hard, and explained to her the harm that could do if children began too early to learn merely by memorizing individual characters. She stopped rather reluctantly and had to be content to know that there was nothing wrong with my brain, happily concluding that I was intelligent.

It was very different after we returned from China. Because my father had sent me to an English school, he decided to teach me classical Chinese himself. Each evening, we sat together after dinner to read simple texts. My father wanted me to learn a language that was not spoken and rarely used except in formal documents. He taught me to remember characters in short sentences, how they were pronounced, and what they meant in the past compared with when used colloquially today. My father believed that the *baihua* vernacular would be easy to master when one had learnt enough classical Chinese, including how to write it. He was therefore reluctant for me to use the standard textbooks used in the Chinese schools. He admired efforts of men like Ho Shih-an 何世庵 (father of my friend Ho Peng Yoke 何丙郁, who later became a historian of Chinese science) who ran private classes in classical Chinese at the time. But he did not send me to study with him because Mr Ho taught the classics in Cantonese.

My father began with the traditional *Sanzi jing* (三字经 Three-Character Classic) and the *Qianzi wen* (千字文 Thousand Character Text) but then turned to the *Xinguowen* (新国文 New National Language) textbooks devised early in the 20th century. These texts were in literary Chinese and included numerous stories about famous Confucian literati, men like Kong Yong 孔融 and Sima Guang 司马光 whose behaviour when young was exemplary. They were the Chinese equivalent of Washington who could not tell a lie and King Alfred and the cakes. Language mastery was thus tied closely to lessons on moral excellence. I accepted that as normal and assumed that the Chinese, American and British peoples shared the same ideas about what was right and wrong.

It soon became clear that learning in this way was not enough. In my school, I was learning different subjects five hours each day five times each week. That way, I was building a vocabulary of English words that described ideas and objects not covered at all in the ancient Chinese texts. I also needed modern Chinese words, so my parents decided to send me to Chinese school in the afternoons. I was nine years old when they bought me a bicycle so that I could ride to a private school nearby in New Town. There I was introduced to words that better matched those that I was learning in my English school.

But my Chinese world was a very small one. The other children in the private school came from the town. Our classroom was a room in a shop-house. We had one teacher, we all met when class started and left when it ended. I realized later why our family was different. It was in part because my parents had no interest in becoming local, but also because we went to the town only to shop or go to the cinema and did neither often. My parents' only close friends were the Wu family who lived on the other side of town by the railway tracks. Mr Wu Yuteng 吴毓腾 was my father's immediate boss and was given a government house near the Education Office. He and his wife both came from Shanghai and, in addition to Shanghainese, spoke *guoyu*. Mrs Wu loved to play mahjong and invited my parents every weekend to make a foursome.

I remember our visits as happy moments in my life. When we arrived in Ipoh, the Wu family consisted of three children. The eldest Ti Hsien 迪先 was several years older and much admired by all of us for the skills he had in making model airplanes. The second Ti Hua 迪华 was our leader in whatever games we played. The youngest was a girl, Ti He 迪和. She was a few months older and I called her elder sister. There were three later additions and I enjoyed being called elder brother by the younger ones. As an only child, becoming friends with the Wu children was the nearest thing to having brothers and sisters of my own. In 1937, Mr Wu's sister Mrs Zhou, Wu Junyi 吴君亦, came with her five children, a boy and four girls, to escape the Japanese invasion. Now were two more children older than me, Zhou Shaohai 周绍海 and Zhou Rongyu 周容与, for me to look up to and hear them tell us about the great city of Shanghai. Curiously, although all the children could speak Mandarin, we often spoke in Cantonese to one another, and the five newcomers who arrived from Shanghai were led to do the same. Cantonese was the dominant language of the shops. Outside government offices, few people in Ipoh understood English, and local *pasar* (bazaar) Malay was the other common language used.

We visited the Wu house in a rickshaw on Sundays and spent the day with them. The children made our own toys and also taught one another the games we learnt in our respective schools, ranging from fighting spiders in matchboxes, to kicking Chinese shuttlecocks and to flying kites. Most of all, we invented games that fully used the large garden that they had and did much hiding and seeking.

One unexpected lesson I learnt came from these regular visits. Each time we went to their home, we would cross a small bridge, passing an elegant Hindu temple and a cave in a limestone outcrop that was used as a Daoist temple. Every now and again, when we passed by, there would be crowds attending ceremonies in one or the other. I was curious to know what it meant to take part, but my parents never stopped to join them.

That made me notice that there were in town many other temples and a few churches and mosques. I saw some with many people praying in them and others covered with incense smoke. My parents made clear to me that they regarded all religious activities as superstitions that had nothing to do with us. I also noticed that none of my parents' friends visited temples or churches and that they too had nothing in their homes to do with religion. When asked to explain, my mother spoke reverentially of our ancestors and told me why she had deep respect for elders in my father's family. We did nothing because we were far away from the family's sacred sites and tablets. However, this did little to help me understand why other people demonstrated their beliefs so openly. But it implanted in me a scepticism towards whatever I thought was not obviously rational.

In retrospect, I accepted that my family's idea of being Chinese was Confucian with deep roots in China's ancient history. This was central to the family's literati background. While that did not stop our family members from admiring Laozi 老子 and Zhuangzi 庄子 and studying Buddhist sutras, priority in that elitist tradition was for young males to be educated to become loyal servants of the emperor-state according to ideals laid down by Confucius and his disciples. Their links with official authority and local social leadership kept most of them distinct from the people whom they were expected to lead, educate and sometimes govern. Thus they saw the various popular ritual and spiritual practices as cultural traits that should be tolerated but not embraced. Their sense of concern towards those in need of help was drawn from principles that demanded rectitude and a kind of distance that kept them apart. I grew up to learn that our family's separateness from other Ipoh Chinese was not only because we lived away from the town but also had its source in the structure of traditional Chinese society.

The World from Green Town

THE OLD TOWN of Ipoh was built at a bend of the Kinta River with impressive government offices, banks and commercial houses. It had the railway station, the Anglican church, the English club, the *padang* where games like cricket and rugby were played, and a few short streets of shops. There were two boys' schools run by Christian missions: the Catholic St Michael's Institution and the Anglo-Chinese School of the Methodists, and also two Chinese primary schools.

Our side of town, on the other side of the river, was New Town, where Chinese retail shops flourished. This was also where the General Hospital was built as well as five large schools: Anderson School established by the state government, the Catholic Convent and the Anglo-Chinese Girls' School that taught in English, and two Chinese high schools, Yuk Choy 育才中学 for boys and Perak Girls' 霹雳女中 for girls. Malay primary schools were in neighbouring kampongs. New Town was also home to the New Market by the river and most of the town's cinemas, and several grand Chinese homes sited along the road to the tin mines and rubber estates and towns further east and south. Near the General Hospital and behind the Convent were government quarters, a place called Green Town. That was where we lived from 1931 to 1941, and again from early 1946 to the middle of 1947.

Our family was an oddity in Green Town. My father was known to have come from Dutch lands, a sojourner-educator and, uniquely, a graduate of a university in China. He was the only person there who worked with Chinese schools and spoke *guoyu* and English, but no Malay and none of the Chinese dialects. Green Town was an exclusive place built to house non-European government officials. Living around our house was a mix of Malays, Chinese, Eurasians and people from Ceylon and British India.

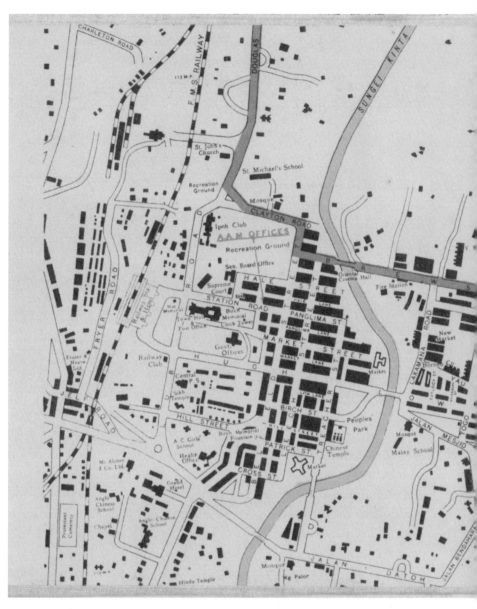

This Automobile Association of Malaya map of Ipoh dates back to 1936. My old Green Town house is circled in the upper right corner. Map of Ipoh (Courtesy of National Archives of Singapore).

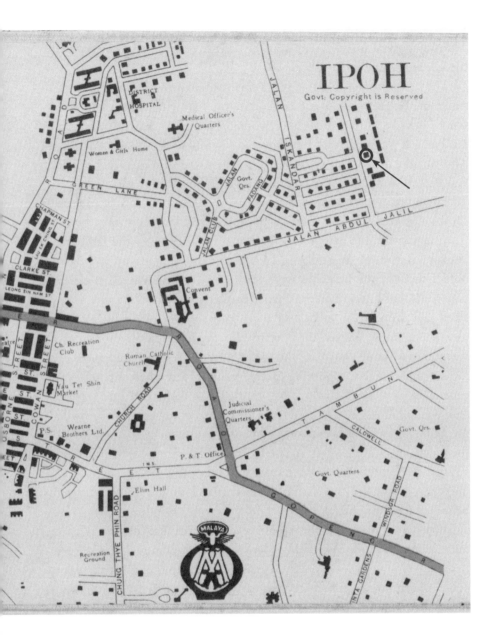

IPOH

Govt. Copyright is Reserved

They all worked for different branches of the government, but none of the Chinese there spoke any *guoyu*.

The house we were allotted was a small public works building, painted standard black-and-white and built on short pillars with a Malay kampong touch. It had a sitting room and two bedrooms, each with a bathroom. At the back was a ten-yard long covered corridor and a walled courtyard. The corridor led to the kitchen, where there was also a servant's room and a small storehouse. We had our meals in the corridor area.

There was a large garden that was marked out by a row of hibiscus shrubs all round. We had three coconut trees and four fruit trees, two of them rambutan, one mangosteen and one durian. One of the rambutan trees was very large and tall and I loved to climb it as far up as I dared until I thought the branches were too thin. Every season, all the trees bore fruits, but I never had the chance to eat the durian. The fruits would ripen and drop in the middle of the night, and our neighbours would pick them up whenever they heard the thud of durian dropping. I sometimes woke up and heard the patter of feet each time it happened. By the morning, there was nothing on the ground. Here I had another early experience of China's shadow. My mother was convinced that tropical fruit was unhealthy. She refused to let me eat any of it when I was growing up. I did surreptitiously eat some rambutan and mangosteen and found them delicious. As that gave me pleasure and did me no harm, it planted the first seed of serious doubt about my mother being always right.

When I was five, my father decided that I should go to Maxwell School, a small English primary school next to his Education Office. He persuaded my mother that that would be all right because they could teach me Chinese at home. My father loved English literature and regretted that he had started learning the language late. He thought this was a good opportunity for his son to start early to master this useful language. It was a strange thing for him to have done. His boss, Mr Wu, and all his friends working in Chinese education sent their children to Chinese schools. My mother argued against it. But he was confident that he was right and registered me with the school. During my first year there, he would take me to school on his bicycle before going to work next door.

That was how I began adjusting to life in two worlds. I was an oddity in my parents' circle because I was the only child who attended an English

Our Green Town house was built to a standard plan by the Public Works Department.

school. On the other hand, the children of Green Town who found me odd because my family was so unmistakably Chinese now thought I was less so. Apart from the few who went to a Malay school, the bulk of them also went to English schools. Once I could speak English, I could join them in play.

Starting at Maxwell School was also convenient. My father brought me there every morning and, at noon, he would take me home for lunch before returning to work. I cannot remember much of the school except that Mrs Francis, a dark-haired matronly English woman, was my Primary One teacher. She taught me the alphabet, corrected my pronunciation and encouraged me to read aloud. She noted that my birth certificate was in Dutch and that I could only speak Chinese and gave me a lot of attention. Most of my class came from homes where English was spoken. The Chinese boys came largely from local-born Baba families, and spoke English along with a mixture of Hokkien and Malay. The Indian boys were from families who had come from Ceylon or British India and knew English well, while the Eurasians spoke English as their first language. There were no Malay boys at the school because they attended their own private madrasahs or public Malay primary schools. Because everyone

That's me aged seven or eight, in school uniform.

spoke English in school all the time, I quickly learnt to use the basics of the language.

After a few months there, the school gave me permission to go with my parents to visit family in China, and I was away for about two months. After I came back, I did well enough in class to continue to Primary Two. Maxwell School was then joined to Anderson School, the government English school located near Green Town and thus much nearer to our house. My father arranged for me to be taken to school by Mrs Navaratnam, who lived at the other end of our street. She and her eldest daughter both taught at Anderson School and went together every morning by rickshaw. I walked to their house and sat in the rickshaw on a small stool at their feet. They had the same rickshaw puller come each morning so the four of us was a regular sight on the way to school. Mrs Navaratnam also became my class teacher when I went on the next year to Standard One. She spoke in English to me each morning and told my father that I was a quick learner. I remember her as the teacher I most enjoyed learning from.

My Primary Two teacher was Miss Widdowson. She was petite and fair-haired and a sticker about speaking correct English. She did not allow us to speak the Malayan English patois that schoolboys used and scolded us if we spoke any of the local languages. My class now included a few Chinese from the town who spoke Cantonese and I remember some of them being fined five cents each time they spoke that language in school. Miss Widdowson provided many storybooks for us to read, and my English improved. But the stories were mostly about children in England, and their lives and exploits were very different from ours. This added one more social layer to those that I already had to live with. My classroom world and the worlds of the different communities of Ipoh town were quite different from the life I shared with my parents and their Chinese teacher friends. The English life I gleaned from the books I read now gave me one more dimension to think about.

Schooldays provided an enclosed world that stood both for discipline and routine, in which one was with friends whose home background was irrelevant and whose lives out of school was of no interest. The times at home and away from school could not be more different. At home, my mother led me into a different social enclosure where every relationship was spelt out and explained, especially those to do with members of our extended family in China. My father was distant during the day in his world of teachers and their problems but, in the evening, was caring about my education in Chinese. After we returned from China in late 1936, he started my evening classes.

Learning in different worlds was never dull. It was daunting to be formally taught together with thirty or more other boys in the class, competing for our teacher's attention and graded to show how much has been learnt. At Anderson School, I was part of such a highly structured school. It had a limited intake of pupils, one class for each standard and each occupied a classroom to itself. What was special, however, was that the school had two separate classes for Malay boys who had finished studies at Malay primary schools in the kampongs nearby. This caught my attention because I had not seen any Malay boys in school before. I was conscious that they were at the school but, until my fifth year in the school, did not meet any of them. We were told that they were scholarship boys who had finished studying at Malay primary schools.

They spent two years catching up with their English before they joined the school's regular Standard Five class. They were older boys who stayed in a hostel supervised by English and Malay teachers. They studied and trained together and we admired the way they helped the school win many awards in inter-school and state sporting events.

Their presence highlighted our mixed community backgrounds, the peculiar product of British colonial power. I did not understand then why the Malay boys were treated differently and no one offered to explain. Years later, in 1941, when I got to know the Malays who joined us in Standard Five, I found them friendly but realized how they still felt a little separate from the rest of us. They had not shared the years of growing up together that the rest of the class had enjoyed but were more like newcomers who had to make an effort to fit in. We did not know what they thought of us as children of people who had come to their Malay state because of British policies but seem to have taken ownership of the school. It later became a question that I realized had long been in my mind for which I had not found the answer. I had hardly begun to know them before the Japanese invaded Malaya. After that, we were all separated and I did not see my classmates until the British returned and the school reopened in September 1945.

Most of my classmates in primary school returned to the school after the war. I had taken for granted that I was the only one who was set to return home to leave Malaya and return to China. It was only decades later that I discovered that there were others who quietly left for their homes in Ceylon (Sri Lanka) and Madras. Some graduated from Indian universities and settled in England or Australia. I met some of them later and was interested to learn how those from British India and Ceylon had little trouble moving between their homes in southern Asia and the Western world. I then found that many local Chinese whose ancestors had come earlier to the Nanyang also had a similar facility between two or more worlds. By that time, I discovered that I too had been conditioned to be able to do the same.

When I entered Anderson School in 1937, we followed a syllabus that was modified from that used in England but common to all the lands controlled by British imperial officials around the world. I did not appreciate the significance of this effort to get us to share a colonial identity because I was myself trying to adjust to the several distinct worlds in and out of school. Years later, when I visited other former British colonies, now members of the Commonwealth, I discovered that those of our generation had read the same books and shared some of the ideas in them. But, at the time, the only certainty was that, with my parents coming from there, China was my home and I would be returning soon.

I had started, of course, in the mainstream of colonial education. I did well. After Primary Two, I went from Standard One to Two, skipped most of Standard Three to jump to Four after one term, and was in Standard Five after only four years. My teachers were either Ceylonese or Indian. In Standard Two was Mr Sabaratnam from Ceylon whose nephew was in my class and we were good friends. Mr Krishnan I really liked, but he taught me for only one term in Standard Three. There were four others from Standards Four and Five: Mr Morais also from Ceylon, Mr Narain Singh from the Punjab, a very cheerful teacher from Bengal Mr Sen Gupta, and Mr Sinniah three of whose many children were later my university mates in Singapore. I did have one Malay teacher, Mohamed Zain who taught us geography with great verve and one Chinese, Mr Chin, who taught art and carpentry.

School was not demanding. Apart from arithmetic and the English language, I never felt I learnt much. We were taught nothing about Ipoh or the state of Perak apart from the fact that there was a Malay sultan and that some of us were technically his subjects. This was borne out when we were taught to show our respect to the sultan's representative, usually the Raja Muda, heir to the throne, or the Raja Bendahara, third in succession, who presided over our annual sports meet and gave away the prizes.

We certainly learnt nothing about the neighbouring lands that were not in British hands, and I do not remember China and Japan ever being mentioned except in passing to note the times when British ships were dominant off the coasts of those countries. What we did know was the extent of the British Empire, all the places marked in red on the maps on display. Apart from that, we were encouraged to take part in the scout movement and in athletic sports. I was keen to take part but had no talent or enthusiasm for either. I was also aware that our art and carpentry teacher was very serious about talent because he was so disappointed to discover that I could not draw.

When I reached Standard Five in 1941, the school was made keenly aware of the war in Europe that had begun in 1939. By that time, we were conscious how much Britain was embattled at home and knew that its vast empire was now in difficulties. I recall seeing our senior schoolmates marching up and down as cadets-in-training, and some of them were known to have joined the local volunteer corps and practiced for battle with imaginary enemies. In the life that I had away from my school, I had, of course, been aware of the war in China since 1937 and realized that the Sino-Japanese war was of little interest among my schoolmates. Thus when Britain was at war, I never felt involved in the exercises to show loyalty to the British. At the end of 1941, just after finishing my Standard Five examinations, the Japanese invaded Malaya and the first bombs fell in Ipoh. It was clear that at last the two wars had converged. Thus the several worlds I lived in were brought together and everyone faced the same fate. But that was also when I left the school that had been central to my formal learning since 1936 and was suddenly introduced to life in another world.

A Taste of China

I DO NOT remember much about our trip to China in 1936. What I know comes mainly from what my mother told me, reinforced by the few photographs taken by my uncle when we were in Taizhou. I have vague images of cities like Singapore, Hong Kong and Shanghai and of being on a large passenger ship. But I cannot recall how we got to Taizhou and, apart from calling on many relatives, what we did there. My mother told me how happy my grandparents were to see me and how well behaved I was when I met all our relatives, apart from an embarrassing incident when, at a ceremony before our ancestral tablets, I climbed on the back of my elder cousin. Although my grandfather was indulgent and did not complain, my mother felt guilty for having not brought me up properly.

I mention this here because it was one of the reasons why she told me so much more about my father's family afterwards. She was determined that I understood that my ancestors had a distinguished lineage. My father never talked to me about family and personal matters. It was left to my mother to tell me where our family came from, about my ancestors from northern China, and why my paternal great-grandparents moved south. In contrast, she told me little about her own family and it was many years later that I found out more about their origins. She was content that I knew that hers was an arranged marriage between good families. I thought all this was normal until much later when I discovered that young people now married for love. That led me to wonder how my parents had adapted to each other so well and lived together with such affection and mutual respect. It opened my mind to the possibility that not everything began with love and that love could go on growing after marriage.

My father worked long days and regularly travelled outside Ipoh to inspect schools far away. I normally only saw him at dinner, after which he taught me basic Chinese and went on to practice his calligraphy and asked me to watch. Now and then, he would take me along when he visited his friend's bookshop in town. He bought me children's books in Chinese and boys' magazines in English, and some news magazines in Chinese for my mother. It was also the time when he would collect his British Sunday papers. What struck me most was how eagerly my mother waited for the magazines that gave her news of events in China, especially the politics of the Chinese civil war and the Japanese incursions in Central and South China.

While my father was happy to hear from my teachers that my English was improving, he never spoke English to me. I knew he could because he worked with English officials in the Education Office, but I never knew how well he spoke the language. Years later I discovered that he wrote very correct English and had a fine grasp of English grammar and idiom, but he never spoke the language with me and I rarely heard him utter a word in English. It was much later when he met my friends from the University of Malaya and talked briefly with them that I realized that he spoke English well.

Those trips I made with him to the bookshop were special treats. There I appreciated that he was comfortable in two complex language worlds and realized that even his English world was in two parts: the public part he used to meet the needs of his office and the private part he turned to in order to follow literary tastes and trends in Britain. All this made him a much more complex man than I understood at the time. Even till this day, whenever I think about him, I know I have never fully appreciated many facets of his life.

In the middle of 1937, the event my parents feared came to pass. War between Japan and China began in earnest. After the incident at Marco Polo Bridge outside Beijing, the Japanese attacked Shanghai; soon afterwards, their troops pushed towards the capital city where many thousands of civilians were killed in what was called the rape of Nanjing. As expected, the Chinese army was no match for the Japanese and the Nationalist leader, Chiang Kai-shek, withdrew deep into the interior to Chongqing. My parents were anxious for their families in towns north of the Yangzi that were soon overrun by the Japanese. What was worse, news came that one of the Nationalist leaders, Wang Ching-wei, returned to Nanjing to collaborate with the Japanese and set up an alternative Nationalist government there. His was no more than a puppet government but it now controlled the counties where our families were. There was nothing my parents could do except to keep on sending money to help, somewhat relieved that the money reached them. But they were deeply embarrassed that the family lived under that Japanese-dominated regime and never mentioned this to anyone. They also made sure that I understood that Wang Ching-wei's surname was not the same as ours and that I should make that clear to anyone who asked about it.

With this war, I became increasingly conscious of being so obviously Chinese at my school. The contrast between what my parents talked about at home and among their friends and what concerned my teachers and fellow pupils in school could not be starker. Our teachers did talk about Britain and the Empire facing tensions in Europe, but there was no mention of the war in China, nor what that might mean for us in the region. Even my school friends who were Chinese did not talk about that war.

My parents followed the events in China closely and supported the Chinese in the town who began to raise funds for the war effort. My mother joined the women's organizations that held events to collect money for the cause. She sometimes allowed me to go with her to attend functions where there were emotional displays of patriotism. I was thus introduced to the elements of nationalism framed in the context of a war when one's country was in retreat. I recall the mixture of resignation, anger and defiance that I associated with anything to do with China, feelings that stayed with me for many years.

I also remember listening to my father telling my mother about the Chinese schools in Perak state that were actively supporting the Nationalists in China. Sometimes, he would also refer to the underlying confusion in the community. There were among its KMT or Guomindang members those who supported Chiang Kai-shek and others who sided with Wang Ching-wei. As for those who sympathized with the opposition parties, including the Chinese Communist Party, there was also considerable debate about how best to work together to support the China Salvation Movement. I listened to my parents without understanding the finer differentiations among the local

Chinese. It was nonetheless my introduction to the elements of national politics. I did not know it at the time, but my parents' conversations had laid the foundations of an interest in political affairs that would surface later in my life.

The Japanese war on Chinese soil dragged on for years. It did not much affect the time I spent with my school friends, with whom I continued to enjoy studying and playing right through that period. It was only when I was home listening to my parents talking that I felt that the ongoing war was really about us.

After 1937, my parents began taking me to cinemas to see patriotic films. I do not remember how many we saw, but one that I saw in 1938 left a very deep impression. This was Babai zhuangshi (八百壯士 The 800 Heroes), a film showing how the opening battle of Shanghai in late 1937 ended in retreat. I joined everyone in the cinema at the end of the film to cheer the heroes who fought bravely before they abandoned the large warehouse that they had been desperately defending. However, something troubled me. The survivors had to cross the river to safety and the bridge was held by British troops. I asked my father what were the British doing on the other side of the Suzhou River. From his answer, I received my first history lesson about modern China. He explained that Britain was not at war with Japan and could not help China. All they could do was to stop the fighting that was close to their properties in the international concession south of the river.

He did not explain further, so I pressed my mother to tell me more. She was no historian but had read her magazines closely enough to give me the standard Chinese version of the two Opium Wars and the role of the British in China's downfall. That was what I would have learnt had I gone to Chinese school, not from the textbooks used in Malaya but from the teachers, who wanted their students to know what they thought of the British, and from fellow students who related what their parents and elder brothers believed. I had heard fragments of the story from conversations between my parents and their friends, but no one had offered a lineal account of how Western imperialism brought China to its knees.

This reminded me that our hometown Taizhou that I had visited earlier was very different from the city of Shanghai. My mother explained that Shanghai was built along the lines of cities like London and Paris, and that the greater part of it was run by the British and the French. She told me that everything modern in China came from that city, including the newspapers and magazines that she read. Shanghai was the model that Chinese leaders used to project China's future, and Chinese businesses there were catching up with Europe. Chinese companies were trying to produce everything that the country needed and wanted Chinese people to buy more from them, but they had to compete with manufactures from the West, and most of all, with the Japanese factories located in Shanghai, whose goods were cheaper and of better quality. With Japan and China now at war, my mother pointed to the efforts in Ipoh to persuade its people to boycott Japanese goods. She described how the boycotts led to violence when some Chinese shops refused to join the boycotts because so much of their business depended on their sale of Japanese products. I never saw the violence, but did hear that the local police sometimes intervened to protect the errant shops from being attacked by fervent patriots.

Thereafter, I listened more carefully to my mother when she talked about going home to China one day. It was now a place that had become more real. I began to identify with it not through the traditional texts my father loved but by catching in my mind's eye the vivid descriptions of war and devastation that my mother gave me. I also became more attentive to other war or patriotic films my parents took me to see. None had the same impact as The 800 Heroes, but I did find one of them memorable. This was sometime in 1940 or 1941 when the film Yue Fei (岳飞 The General Yue Fei) came to Ipoh. It was the story of the Song dynasty general who defied orders to fight the Jurchen invaders of northern China. My father loved it and introduced me to the famous poem *Manjianghong* (满江红 The River All Red) that Yue Fei was thought to have written. It was a moving poem the opening lines of which still leave a tingle in me. It expressed something close to the national sentiments that had now entered my life. The song composed for it became very popular and it remains one of my favourite songs. I learnt to sing the version popular at the time but never knew who composed that version. It is one of the few wartime songs I can still sing today.

My parents began to take me to the cinema more often and I looked forward to each of the films that we saw. I could understand why my mother came to dislike going to some of the Chinese films. She thought too many of them were tearjerkers that made the audience very sad and she thought real life was sad enough. For me, I particularly liked the films that produced popular songs. I liked those sung by Zhou Xuan 周璇 and Bai Guang 白光 and learnt to sing them along with my childhood friends of the Wu family. One of Zhou Xuan's most successful films, Malu Tianshi (马路天使 Street Angel), stayed in my mind for years.

When I saw the film The 800 Heroes, war in Europe was imminent. My schoolteachers began to talk about the possibility that, with Britain, France and Netherlands engaged on that continent, Japan would be tempted to look south and threaten their colonies. I do not recall the discussions being very serious but there were by then some reason for anxiety. Once war began in Europe, talk in the classroom included the Sino-Japanese conflict. But the concern was not about China but that it might spread to Malaya.

The Malayan government was determined to keep everything as normal as possible. Local British officials did become more sympathetic towards China Salvation events and I recall how my mother was drawn to take part in more of them. My father, however, was not one to engage in political debate and show his feelings. He had the task of keeping an eye on school activities that were politicized among different Chinese factions. He said little and kept a low profile while trying to discourage school boards and principals from turning schools into political arenas. He did this because he believed that his responsibility was to provide good education for all who wanted to study and did not want the pupils to be too distracted. Although he attended many community fund-raising events and talked to everyone who sought his advice, he never spoke publicly about China politics.

When I was older and knew him a little better, I realized that my father had a keen sense of duty and great self-control. His strict Confucian upbringing made him dislike the idea of contentious parties and factions fighting against legitimate authority. As an education officer, he sought to be above all that, although he told my mother how difficult that was and how painful it was to be caught in some of the struggles between local dissenting groups that were constantly going on.

He continued to teach me Chinese and was angry when I failed to memorize essays or poems that he considered relatively straightforward. At the same time, he encouraged me to improve my English and even took me to see English films. He was fond of those with historical themes and my mother also loved them. I remember her being especially moved by films like Mary of Scotland and The Private Lives of Elizabeth and Essex. She surprised me by her familiarity with the life of Queen Elizabeth and revealed that she had thought a lot about the role of women in history. I began to hear about the Empress Lu 吕后 who helped the founder of the Han dynasty, and the popular story of Hua Mulan 花木兰, who dressed as a man to take her father's place when he was conscripted. When the film Mulan Congjun (木兰从军 Maiden in Armour or Mulan Joins the Army) came to Ipoh, she loved it so much she took me to see it a second time. I was so taken by Chen Yunshang 陈云裳, the young woman who played Mulan, that I always saw her face whenever the name Mulan was mentioned. I heard later that she gave up acting to marry a doctor in Shanghai but was happily surprised to find that when I met her in Hong Kong some fifty years later, her looks still conjured up the name of Mulan.

My mother was not a feminist but very conscious of the woman's place in traditional China. The Mulan story led her to tell me of the dreadful practice of binding women's feet that severely limited their ability to be active. She told me Mulan could do what she did, and someone like Empress Wu Zetian 武则天 during the Tang Dynasty could become so powerful, because their feet were free. But from the tenth century onwards, Chinese women were made to bind their feet, and over the centuries the pressure grew stronger in most families to get the girls to make their feet even smaller. My mother was particularly scathing about the Chinese when she came to the Manchu conquest of China during the 17th century and pointed out that the barbaric Manchus treated their women better. Although they learnt much from the Chinese, they left their women's feet to remain natural.

She also described how close she was to becoming a cripple when she was about ten years old, how her mother cried while supervising the binding and explaining why it had to be done. She then dramatically described the moment when the bindings were taken off and her feet were saved. For this, she emphasized, she was eternally grateful to the revolution in 1911 for the overthrow of the dynastic system that had been so cruel to women. She showed me her feet, pointing to their small size and explaining why they never gained their full size. She then told me that was why she respected modern Western ideas of progress for the equal status given to women and why she supported the modernizers in the cities who were working to make China prosperous and strong again. I have never been able to separate human progress from the position of women ever since.

My father, however, was consistent in placing great emphasis on the importance of literary skills in the forefront of modernity. He believed that it was those skills that made Chinese civilization great and, ultimately, similar skills are needed to learn the language and thought that made Western civilization progressive and appealing. Therefore, he always encouraged me to read his books and magazines and, whenever possible, see films that were based on famous literary works.

For example, I remember how he introduced me to A Tale of Two Cities, one of the first films he took me to see when I was still in primary school. He prepared me for it by showing me his copy of the book and telling me that I must learn English so that I could read it one day. He then told me the story so that I could enjoy the film. The film left such a strong impression that I have never forgotten the name of the young actor who played David, Freddie Bartholomew. I made it a point to ask to see every film he acted in, and remember telling my mother that he was better than the young actress she thought was adorable, Shirley Temple. Of the films I saw, I was most moved by one called Lloyd's of London, which featured the death of Admiral Nelson after his victory at Trafalgar. That gave me another insight into the idea of patriotism and the feelings that it aroused. Nelson became the English parallel to my Chinese hero Yue Fei, and I have never lost the sense of loss that I felt when he died in the film. To my surprise, in 1954, when I made my first visit to London and stood before Nelson's statue in Trafalgar Square, that feeling overcame me. But I have always felt particularly sad that Nelson was honoured for dying heroically fighting the enemy while the ruler whose kingdom Yue Fei had tried to save had ordered to have him executed.

Through the films I saw, I noticed that, at a very basic level, I was now comfortable in both languages, Chinese and English. It made me feel that my parents' world was coming closer to that of my other world around Anderson School. The parallel lines between the bits of classical Chinese writings I learnt with my parents and the myths and fables of the Mediterranean that were being introduced to us in school might not have met, but they enlarged my view of the world outside Ipoh immeasurably.

Empire's End and Other Spheres

WHEN THE SOUNDS of war grew louder, I thought that the gap between English school and Chinese home would lessen. But I could not help feeling that the sense of separateness remained, and sometimes the gap seemed unbridgeable. School treated us as pupils who more or less belonged to British Malaya and hoped that we would learn to look at Britain with admiration. Home was my parents and their circle, and then extended to a set of networks focused on China. I moved quite freely between the two but only by keeping them apart in my mind, and in what I said and did.

When Britain went to war, our teachers knew that we could not be expected to be patriotic about British efforts to save their troops at Dunkirk, and I understood that. If there was any interest in the European war, it came from those of us who felt that Britain and China were finally on the same side. We did notice that "God save the King" was heard more often on local radio and the anthem began to be played in cinemas before each film. I can remember that our feelings towards that were lukewarm. Years later I realized that some of our teachers were relaxed about the war because they harboured hopes that a weakened Britain would make it easier to end colonialism, and allow India and Ceylon to gain their independence.

In 1941, I was in Standard Five. That was equivalent to the 7th year in school, the last year of primary school. I was ten years old at the beginning of that year and eager to learn from the new set of specialist teachers we were provided in subjects like English and mathematics. There was more English grammar to learn and we were encouraged to write longer and more ambitious essays. We were given poetry to recite, and some of us had chances to act in short and simple plays. A few of us ventured to make short speeches about topics that caught our attention.

In mathematics, we now needed more language skill and more thought and calculation. And we were introduced to some elementary algebra and geometry. Most of us thought that it was still largely a matter of practice and I do not recall any of us being outstanding and additionally curious about the mysteries of numbers.

The geography class was interesting. We were taught simple facts about landforms, climate, crops and agriculture, mining and industry, trade following the flag, the location of ports and cities and I could sometimes relate them to the globe in our classroom. Some of the teachers did urge us to study hard but it did not seem that school policy was to pressure us to excel. For most of the time, we were encouraged to be healthy and compete in the sports field. My closest friends believed that school should be fun.

Elsewhere, everything was more serious. The Chinese schools my father was responsible for were committed to support the war in China. By 1940, their school assemblies were focused on being patriotic as overseas Chinese and, every night at dinner, my father would update my mother and me about the mood in the community. I recall conversations when they talked about some aspects of history, about Sun Yat-sen's aspirations and the role of Chinese abroad in the 1911 revolution, and also efforts thereafter to build a modern nation. My mother, an avid reader of the latest Chinese magazines, would tell us about the course of the war, the desperate needs of people in China and the efforts of her women friends in Ipoh to raise money. On Sundays, when I saw my childhood friends of the Wu and the Zhou families who all went to Chinese schools, they described their activities in school and their efforts to support the Chinese defence forces. The eldest of them who was in the local high school talked about classmates whose brothers had volunteered to fight in China. Several had left to join the Nationalist army and we were especially excited by the story of one of them joining the air force to become a pilot.

Late in 1938, the Wuhan Choir, already famous among the Chinese overseas, arrived in Malaya to raise funds for the war effort in China. They started with Singapore and were visiting all the states with a sizeable Chinese population. When they eventually turned up in Ipoh the next year, they won the hearts of most local Chinese. The choir's leader was already well known to us. He was the composer of "The 800 Heroes", the song I first heard in the film about defending Shanghai and by then extremely popular.

I was too young to gauge whether there were Chinese who were not carried away by the emotional responses around us and did not share the passionate patriotism felt by the rest of the community. My mother alerted me to this by telling me about a few Chinese businessmen who were unwilling to make even a small donation to the war cause. My father was as usual silent about his workplace and I can only guess what his British, Indian and Malay colleagues thought. I was aware that most families of my Chinese classmates at Anderson School were not interested in the Wuhan Choir visit. They were conscious that they lived in what the British described as sovereign monarchies and were uncomfortable that Chinese should be so demonstrative in their enthusiasm for a cause not connected to the British or the Malays. Although the Malay rulers of the states with the most Chinese populations like Perak, Selangor and Negri Sembilan were not in actual control of their states, they probably wondered why their British protectors had allowed such open displays of an alien loyalty.

I had learnt to sing popular Chinese songs from my friends. By this time, we wanted to sing patriotic songs. We had learnt a few from the films we saw but, after hearing the Wuhan Choir perform, the songs became more closely linked directly to the war in China. They included the "Volunteers Marching Song" 义勇军进行曲, later to become the National Anthem of the People's Republic of China; several songs of loss and heroism like "On the Sungari River" 松花江上 about the refugees from Manchuria who lost their homes; and, not least, "China Will Not Die" 中国不会亡, the song of the 800 Heroes of Shanghai. Some evenings, I accompanied my mother to concerts where new songs were introduced, and I learnt to sing them as well. That was when patriotic feelings were reinforced but I was also conscious that it was only a small part of my response to the events unfolding quickly before us.

The Wuhan Choir consisted largely of university students and recent graduates, many of them with a Shanghai background. The Wu family got to know some of the singers and I remember meeting two of the women visiting their home. They had remained behind after the choir returned to China and found work teaching in schools in Perak. When the war ended, they both left for Shanghai. Years later, when Mr Wu's wife died, one of them returned and eventually married Mr Wu. Because my mother got to know her well and she was stepmother to my friends, I was continuously reminded of the Wuhan Choir that left a deep impression on the Chinese in Malaya.

As an only child, I had my mother's full attention, and my father was very protective and deliberate about my education. But he never really explained why he decided to send me to an English school. Many of his friends were critical of his decision. He was, however, very public about his intention to return to China and my mother never failed to prepare me for that day. She even told me, when I asked her why I did not have brothers and sisters like all my friends, that it was because she wanted us to be able to afford to travel home to China when the chance came.

Thus I grew up thinking that we were not normal in Ipoh, and that Ipoh was definitely not our home. Other Chinese in town seemed more settled. They had their own organizations and temples and organized their festivals and social activities regularly. But, apart from those arranged for fund-raising for the defence of China, our family did not join any of them. I was reminded that we were Confucian and believed only in rituals that paid respect to ancestors. Beyond that, we were at most observers. Above all, we were known as the family living only temporarily in Ipoh and always ready to leave.

I remember two conflicting thoughts that troubled me now and again. One was that I liked being in Ipoh. I loved my school and my friends and was not happy at the thought of leaving them. The other was more discomforting. I did believe that China was our real home and loved the music and films that China produced. I was therefore keen to master everything I could to prepare myself to return. Yet I was also drawn to the images of England in my books at school, especially those that dovetailed with those in English writings, notably the schoolboys' magazines that my father encouraged me to read and the stories from English history and literature that were introduced to us in my school.

A temporary resolution came when I was ten years old. This was when my father bought me a beautiful world atlas as a birthday present. I had seen such books in school but never thought they would be exciting to read. But when I had my own copy and began to pore through each map, I was overwhelmed by the sense of discovery and wanted to examine every corner of the globe. My father was surprised when he found me so transfixed by every part of the atlas. After going through some of the pages many times, I felt the urge to list every feature of importance, if only to help me remember them. I started with the countries, cities and provinces, then the islands, oceans and seas, the mountains and valleys, and then the peninsulas, bays, gulfs and capes. After a while, I could visualize the better-known places and where exactly they were in the maps.

My mother noticed that I stopped going out to play with my friends after school. Instead, I went straight to my room after lunch and turned to my atlas. I filled a special exercise book with my lists. I no longer felt burdened by being located in any single place. There was so much to learn beyond China and England, so many places far away from Ipoh. And when I related them to the historical films I saw, especially those about the British empire spread around the world, I found another dimension in life in which there were many interesting times in the past to turn to. With so much space and so much time out there in the five continents, I was filled with wonder at what the world had to offer.

From then on, every time I felt uneasy about who or where I was, I would think about the atlas and my lists. I would then feel a pleasurable calm. I could think of Shanghai and London, Horatio Nelson and Yue Fei, whoever and wherever. All places and people had become knowable. I began to feel that nothing could stand in the way of my learning about them. Looking back, I believe I had accidentally found a way to make my oddity easier to bear. Indeed, I began to feel I was not so different after all.

My Mother Remembers

"My home was originally in the city of Zhenjiang, Jiangsu province. Because of the Taiping Rebellion, my ancestors moved to Dongtai. That was over a hundred years ago. Dongtai was somewhat isolated where modern education was not developed. Thus, although I was brought up in a relatively well-off family with a scholarly background, the family was conservative. It strongly disapproved of women leaving home to study. This meant that I did not have the opportunity to receive higher education, something that, till now, I still regret. At the time I was married at the age of twenty-three, I had no experience at all of managing a household. Servants did all the domestic work for us. In addition, my loving mother shielded me from all this. As a result, I developed the habit of not caring for trifling matters, like not being able to tell the difference between grain and legumes. Fortunately, I later changed my ways and did not end up totally ignorant of household affairs. Before we were married in February 1929, your father and I had never met. Surprisingly our feelings for each other have been good; we have cared for each other, shown each other mutual respect and have gone through hard and sweet times together, and the several decades have passed like a day.

Your father, a graduate from the Southeastern University in Nanjing, was teaching in two schools in Taizhou. The family home was a large one where three generations lived under the same roof. At the time I joined the family, the family had been broken up for several years and your home had only your grandparents, a grand aunt, your uncle (father's brother) and his wife and your aunt (father's sister). I lived with them for several months and felt comfortable and close to them all.

Early in September (1929), I learnt that my maternal grandmother was very ill and went home (to Dongtai) to see her. A few days afterwards, she passed away. I was still there grieving for her when I received your father's letter. It said that his university classmate's father, Mr Qiao Yin-gang (喬蔭岡), who had recommended your father to be the headmaster of the Huaqiao Middle School in Surabaya, told him the formal letter of appointment has arrived together with 300 yuan for travel expenses. It was a time when job opportunities were few and far between. Although this meant leaving home and family, he felt he should accept the offer.

I was to go along. It meant we had to get our things ready to travel quickly. Thus, late in September, we said our farewells and went first to Nanjing. Because 300 yuan was not enough for our tickets, we needed to borrow another 300 yuan from his former classmate, Mr Qiao Yi-fan (喬 一凡). Mr Qiao readily provided us with the sum we needed and gave us a farewell dinner. Indeed, we were moved by his friendship. Your fourth maternal uncle in Nanjing [Mr Ding, my mother's brother or cousin] also invited us to a send-off dinner.

We went to Shanghai to wait for our ship and stayed at the Huizhong 惠中 Hotel. I visited your fourth "aunt" [actually my mother's cousin] whose husband, Mr Yan Yi-fu 严毅甫, was working at the Bank of Communications. They kindly hosted us for dinner. There was also your "uncle", Mr Cao Nan-ping 曹南屏, husband of your father's cousin and a scion of a wealthy family. He was studying at Fudan University and also invited us for dinner. Your uncle, Shao-wen 绍文 [my father's younger cousin] was also studying at Fudan at the time. Your seventh great grand-uncle [my grandfather's uncle] was in Shanghai at the time working for Mr Hu Bi-jiang 胡笔江 as a family tutor. Mr Hu, one of the leading lights in Shanghai's financial sector, greatly respected his integrity and literary skills and had specially appointed him to teach his sons classical Chinese and, with his moral character, be an exemplar for them. Mr Hu certainly had an original view on this matter.

I remember how your seventh great grand-uncle was fond and protective of us and took us to walk round the Great World Centre and have dinner there. Your uncle Shao-wen also came along. For those times fifty years ago, to do that was unusually open-minded. And when we were travelling there by rickshaw, he insisted that the rickshaw I was in be in the middle to ensure that nothing went wrong. You can imagine (how I felt) to have a senior member of the family so careful and thoughtful.

We were a few days at the hotel before we boarded our ship. It was named "Zhi-jia-da" 芝加达. There were two kinds of cabins, first class and third class. It was not docked at the pier but anchored in the middle of the Huangpu River, so could only be reached in small boats. We went on board at night. Being the first time I was boarding a large ship, I was filled with anxiety. On board, men and women were separated. Each cabin had six bunks one on top of the other. In my cabin, all my companions were Guangdong and Fujian compatriots and their dialects were wholly incomprehensible, so you can imagine how depressed I was. In addition, each time the ship reached another port, it would stop to discharge cargo for one or two days. Given that the weather was very hot and the work was noisy, it was really miserable.

We travelled for fifteen days and, at the end of October, reached our destination. Fortunately, the chairman of the school, Mr Zhang Ji-an 张济安, as Chairman of the Chinese Chamber of Commerce, was someone of wealth and influence and highly regarded by the local authorities. He personally came to meet the ship and enabled us to disembark without having to undergo long queues and the humiliating experience of being treated as piglets. We were thus not delayed and the envy of the other passengers.

Mr Qiao Yin-gang had already rented a place for us to stay with two rooms, a hall and a dining room. The monthly rent was 80 yuan. It was located in a quiet and secluded area not far from the school. Each trip to the school by horse-buggy was ten cents. It was really an ideal place in the residential district. But it was really too expensive, and it would be much cheaper for us to live on the school premises. That would also be more convenient for your father's work. So, after two months, we moved into the school grounds.

Only after your father started work at the school and talked in detail with the school board members did he begin to realize the actual conditions of the school. It did not have its own premises nor any endowed funds but depended on raising some 20,000 to 30,000 yuan now and again to pay all its expenses. How could the school sustain itself for long that way? We first saw the splendid building in which the school was housed but found out that the monthly rent was an expensive 400 yuan. There were also charges for water and electricity and other miscellaneous costs. Also, the salaries for teachers were not low. School expenditure depended only on irregular monthly donations and school fees. Each month's income was not enough for half a month's expenses. That meant that what had been donated could not last more than half a year before the coffers were empty. Even when teachers' salaries were discounted by 20 per cent, there was not enough to pay them.

Furthermore, the family in Taizhou was in financial straits, continually asking for remittances and we were hard put to meet their requests. Your father thought hard about this but was unable to find a solution to the problem. Unsettled, he felt he was unable to do his work well nor help his family. He contemplated resigning but the school was not agreeable. So he could only make greater efforts to tap other sources of funding while cutting down expenses. He added to his workload spending a lot of time and energy to organize a fund-raising fair.

When the fair was about to be opened, I was about to give birth and thus added further to his worries. This being my first baby, there was considerable pain from morning to night and still the baby was not born. Eventually, the doctor assisted birth and the baby weighed about eight pounds or so. It was a lovely baby. Both your father and I were first-time parents, so could not help but be somewhat tense. I was in poor health and stayed two weeks before leaving the hospital. Back at home, you cried every evening and wanted to be carried. Our colleague, Mr Zheng, told us that it was good and harmless for a child's health to cry for twenty minutes without stopping. So we followed advice and we all surrounded your bed to watch you cry. After less than twenty minutes, you stopped and never cried again. The strangest thing is that a baby less than two weeks old seemed to understand what that meant, something that has made me wonder to this day.

Because I was young and knew nothing about looking after my health, I did not know what to take to help me recover my strength. At the time, I could not find patent medicine for my needs and it was several months before I gradually recovered. The hospital specialized in obstetrics and rather well-known, but it was quite far from the school, some thirty li 里 (about ten miles) away. Your father took time to come and see me every day, so you can imagine how fully engaged he was. Fortunately, the fund-raising fair was quite successful. It raised some 20,000 yuan and the school was able to pay the teachers all that they were owed. There was not much left after that, so the question of how to go on funding the school remained uncertain.

At the end of the year, one of the teachers was to return to China. Your father organized a dinner to send her off and insisted that I go with him. You were not yet three months then. We had no one to look after you because our Malay maid only worked during the day and went home every evening. The only thing to do was to ask one of the school workers to carry you to the dinner. We did not notice that the worker carried you in the open under the eaves. After dinner, we found you had caught cold and developed a high fever. You also had difficulty breathing and could not sleep. Your father and I had to take turns to carry you. It was a serious illness because you were unable to drink any milk for four days. Fortunately, the doctor diagnosed correctly and you gradually recovered. But, from then on, you frequently suffered from asthmatic relapses. As a result, you did not have a strong constitution and did not really recover from that until your teens. All those years, that was a source of much anxiety for us all.

Considering the economic conditions of many of the huaqiao Chinese in the Dutch East Indies, there were not a few wealthy ones among them. If the school boards were not so divided into factions and were generous in making donations, there would have been more than enough funding to protect Chinese education and build a very good Chinese Middle School. But if that is not what they care about, what can be done?

One day, I was taking a walk with your father and, not thinking about when the train might be passing through, we walked along the tracks. It was only when, as we were walking along, we noted that the gates were being shut that we realized that the train was about to pass. Your father was ahead but I did not panic and calmly and quickly followed him off the tracks. Had I been a minute slow, I could have been killed, that was how dangerous it was. Thinking about the incident afterwards, a lingering fear remained.

Your father was with the school for more than a year. In trying to keep expenses as low as possible, he did not recruit more teachers even when they were needed. Instead, he took on the extra teaching burdens himself. Apart from his administrative duties, he thus had to teach more than twenty hours of class each week. Although this helped to ease the school finances, it was no great help to the future of the school. With such a heavy load of work, it became clear he could not keep this up for long, so he firmly decided to resign. When this was approved, he was in no position to seek another position, nor would it have been easy to find other suitable positions there. Furthermore, the school owed him salary to the sum of 3,000 guilders; if they could have paid him half of that, we would have been grateful. Despite many reminders, the money was not forthcoming because the school board members were not willing to take responsibility for the debt.

At the time, heavy floods struck our home in Taizhou and all roads there were under water. We were unable to send any money back to help the family, and could only wait it out in the school. Although food and lodgings were not a problem, you can imagine how depressed we were. We waited for some three months without any news, not knowing when we could leave.

Suddenly, one day a letter came from one of your father's former colleagues in Singapore, Mr Li Chun-ming 李春鸣, to say that the Education Department in Ipoh in Malaya was looking for someone to fill the post of assistant inspector (of Chinese schools) and suggested that your father give it a try and apply for it. If successful, he will be working with Mr Wu Yu-teng, someone who was also a former colleague at the Huaqiao Middle School in Singapore. Having no alternative, he made the application and it was successful. Fares for the whole family were provided so we were prepared to forego the salary owed. Just before we were about to leave, one of the board members, Mr Lin Sheng-di 林生地, privately gave us 300 yuan and expressed his apologies. Another board member arranged for us to travel on his cargo ship so that we could save on our fares. We were grateful for their gestures of appreciation.

The Dutch East Indies was a clean and well-organized place with many famous historical sites. It was a pity that, although we were there for over two years, we did not visit any of them because we did not have the money and were uncertain how long we would stay. Apart from colleagues at the school, we made only a few friends. Our lives were extremely simple so that, when leaving Surabaya, I did not have many fond memories of it.

The ship we sailed in was not large, carried little cargo and was thus unstable in the open seas. When passing Bandjarmasin, the seas became very rough. Your father and I were both so seasick we were unable to get up from our beds and, like suffering from a great illness, also unable to hold down any food and drink. Fortunately, we had brought with us a wooden cot that could be used as a bed or serve as a chair. Every day, we placed this cot in the middle of the dining hall and put you in it with some biscuits and let you feed yourself. From very young, you were well behaved. You did not cry and were not afraid of strangers. Even when you did not see your parents for the whole day, you did not cry. In the afternoon, I forced myself to get up to take you for your bath and give you milk, and then looked after you until you went to sleep. We did this for three days before arriving in Singapore.

There Mr and Mrs Zhao Xin-hou 赵信侯 came to meet us and helped us with our luggage. Mr Zhao was a friend who had travelled with us when we first came out. We did not stay long in Singapore. That night, we took the night train to Kuala Lumpur and stayed in the home of Mr Lee. His younger brother, Kai-mo 李楷模 was also looking for a job. The next day, your father went to the hospital for a medical examination. The doctor diagnosed a protein problem and said he needed to stay in the hospital for observation. Mr Wu (your father's superior in his new job), who was in KL on official business and about to return to Ipoh, asked me if I was willing to go ahead to Ipoh with him. Because it was not very convenient to stay long in Mr Lee's rather complicated family, I agreed to go ahead to Ipoh.

We arrived in Ipoh by noon and met Mrs Wu for the first time. She struck me instantly as someone who was easy to get along with but somewhat immature. She loved to go out and play mahjong with her friends and did not pay much attention to teaching her children and managing the home, thus neglecting her responsibilities as its head. I stayed at the Wu home for over ten days before your father came to Ipoh. We prepared to move into the house provided for us by buying some simple essentials, like beds, mattresses, furniture, cupboards and chairs, kitchen utensils, all second-hand because the prices were lower. We also bought a bicycle. Altogether it did cost quite a lot. Fortunately, the Board member [in Surabaya] had given us 300 yuan just before we left, and we saved 200 yuan on our fares. This money was most useful. Apart from paying for the basic settling down expenses, we were able to send 100 yuan to Taizhou to help deal with the family's urgent needs.

After troubling the Wu household for so long, we finally completed several kinds of miscellaneous matters and moved to our new home with all the things we had bought. We were helped greatly by Mr and Mrs Wu, and were very moved by that. Viewed by the standards of fifty years ago, the house we moved into was not bad at all. It had two bedrooms and a living room, two bathrooms, a kitchen and a room for the servant. The grounds were spacious and had several fruit trees. The whole area consisted of quarters for civil servants, quiet and neat, and the conditions were really quite ideal. The only problem was the house faced west and the sun in the tropics was too strong. We had to shut all our front doors and windows every day at one o'clock until six o'clock in the evening. Because we did not have machines to expel the heat, this meant that the air in the house did not circulate for several hours. In those days, air-conditioners had not yet been invented; even fans were not common. Now all kinds of equipment are driven by electricity; compared to decades ago, the speed of progress is incalculable. That is what they mean by the past not being as good as the present, although the higher standards of living are still not something everyone can enjoy.

When your father arrived in Ipoh, various countries in the world were gripped by economic panic. This had brought salaries to low levels. He received 120 dollars a month with an annual increment of ten dollars. There was no need to worry about wages not being paid. Also, prices of goods were low and the monthly rent for the house was seven dollars. After sending thirty dollars each month to Taizhou, there was still ninety dollars. Though we did not have spare funds to purchase anything extra, we lived within our means. Our lives were simple and may be considered quiet and comfortable.

Ipoh was the capital of the state of Perak, but it was rather unenlightened. There were no entertainment centres. Its education was not developed. In the whole state, there were over forty Chinese schools but only a few in Ipoh, the rest being located in the villages like traditional private schools. Facilities were poor. Most of them had atap huts for schoolhouses, with one blackboard and a dozen or so old tables and chairs. They had one or two teachers each and some twenty to thirty pupils. Quite a number of them were no more than that. Only a very few were somewhat better provided.

It is hard to describe how difficult it was for your father to get to these schools when he went on his inspection trips. There were no trains or roads for cars to travel on. He had to use wooden sampans to cross the rivers; in the rubber estates, he rode bicycles or walked. By the time he reached the schools, you can imagine how much time and energy he had spent. He did that only so that he could give the teachers a little guidance about teaching methods. That group of teachers had limited training but to be able to perform their tasks and live under such primitive conditions, their spirit of dedication was admirable. Inspiring village children to open their minds to study, their contributions certainly deserve to be honoured.

We had arrived only three months when Diyu 迪宇 was born and (his elder sister) Dihe 迪和 contracted chickenpox. To avoid infecting the newborn baby, Mr Woo discussed with us about sending their servant with Dihe to live with us for a while. Although we knew you were likely to be infected, we could not refuse the request. As expected, after four or five days, you were also infected. The infection was unavoidable for children; it was only a matter of when it happened.

Your father's work was not very busy. Every weekend we went to the Woo's to play mahjong because Mr and Mrs Woo found life somewhat monotonous and wished to while the time away. Your father always felt at heart that this was a waste of time but found it difficult to decline and disappoint them and affect our friendly feelings. On average, we went at least fifty to sixty times each year, spending over ten hours each time. In the ten years we did this, we wasted so much precious time. This was really a pity.

When we settled down to life in Ipoh, I had hoped to learn some English so that I could make use of it. But there was at the time no private tutoring I could turn to. We found out from friends that the

Convent provided an afternoon class teaching English. With my little English, I could fit into the Standard Three class, except that my spoken English was quite inadequate. I also felt that I was really too old to be in the class with the young children. In addition, you were young and naughty and could not really be left to a servant to look after. Furthermore, your father had no intention to stay long there. For all these several reasons, I missed the opportunity to study. Even today, when I think about it, I feel a great regret.

After a year or so, we began to have more friends, like Mr Xu Kuibo 许逵伯, Mr Yin Pengling 尹彭龄 and Mr Wang Shoumin 王寿民, they were fellow provincials of Jiangsu and Zhejiang. During their school holidays, they would come and visit us. We also made many other friends from among school board directors and teachers. But there was little contact normally, and we met only when there were meetings about public business and other social occasions. At the Woo's home, we also met Mr Zeng Zhiqiang 曾智强 and Mr Dai Shulin 戴澍霖, and they were our earliest friends. About two years later, Mr Li Kaimo 李楷模, at a time when it was normally necessary to be introduced before one could get a job, brought several teachers from his hometown in Nantong [in Jiangsu province] to Malaya to look for jobs. This was a very bold step and his enthusiasm was admirable. Coming with them were three husband and wife couples, Mr Xu Jishi 许济时 who became head of the Chinese school at Jiwuying (吉勿营=积莪营, Chenderiang), Mr Shao Qi 邵琦, who was headmaster of the school in Kroh, and Mr Li Weihan 李维汉, who became headmaster at Teluk Anson. At least they all found regular positions. Mr Xu and Mr Shao were both conscientious and responsible, but Mr Li did not have a good character and could not avoid getting into trouble. During the vacations, they would come to Ipoh to visit and talk. All three schools were in areas that your father was responsible for and their coming added several fellow provincials among our friends.

Once our female servant caught cold washing her hair; her whole body shook and her face changed colour, giving me a fright. I wanted to leave the house to inform one of her friends and asked you to look after the house and wait for me to return. The doors were all open at the time. You were playful and went off to play with your friends.

Your father came to work in Ipoh without intending to stay long. Although life was calm and orderly, he always felt his work did not have much meaning for him. He often felt unease whenever he thought of having received his country's training without having done anything in return. But what could be done when there was no way he could serve? Having hastily come to Ipoh and been there for over three years and with his contract due to end, he was expected to decide whether to stay or leave. At that time, the international situation was getting tenser each day when war could break out any moment. Japan bullied our country for years. Although arms preparation was not enough, it was more than anyone could bear. It was feared that war would be forced upon us anytime. In addition, it was uncertain whether jobs could be found at home, how then could we support the old and the young at home? We thought about all this again and again and could not sleep for three nights. Finally, we decided to give up the job and leave.

The local government was very surprised but respected our wish. But a few days later, we received a personal letter from your seventh great-uncle that analyzed all the factors and argued that your father should not rashly resign. But the letter of resignation had already been sent and one should not go back on one's word. Coincidently, and fortunately, the inspector of (Chinese) schools in Selangor, Mr Liang Changling 梁长岭, had recommended to the government that your father be kept on for another half year because the end-of-the-year unified examination was a very busy time and he was needed to help mark the examination papers. Your father agreed. Not long after, someone in the Inspectorate came personally to ask your father to re-consider. Your father took advantage of this to turn around and continue in his job.

But we had been away abroad for over seven years and missed our family greatly, so we asked for home leave. Although we had been working outside for so many years, we had no savings and had to ask Mr Woo to lend us 300 dollars for travel expenses, to be paid back with two months' salary. In August 1936 we boarded a P & O ship [SS Rawalpindi]. Although we were travelling second class, it was not bad because the three of us shared a cabin.

By chance, we met Professor Mei Guangdi 梅光迪 with his whole family on board. They were returning home from Europe and passing through Singapore. He had been your father's teacher when he was studying at Southeastern University. To meet again after not having seen each other for ten years gave your father great pleasure indeed.

The ship was large and the seas were calm, so we did not suffer any seasickness. After a week, we arrived in Shanghai. Waiting for us at the docks were your uncle, Mr Yan Zhongfu 严中甫 [mother's cousin's husband, related to Mr Yan Yi-fu 严毅甫, mentioned earlier], your aunt Jingyi 静仪 (biaoyi 表姨, mother's cousin) [she was also my mother's closest friend], your aunt Peiyu 佩玉 (姨母, mother's sister), your uncle Shaowen 绍文 (father's cousin). When we landed, we were shocked to hear that your seventh great-grand uncle died a few days earlier and his coffin had been sent back to Taixian (now Taizhou). This sudden bad news caused us great sadness.

That night, Mr Yan invited us to a welcome dinner. After that, we were invited to a Peking opera performance but, bearing in mind your great-grand uncle's recent passing, we did not attend but returned early to our hotel, the same Huizhong we stayed in (in 1929). You were then not quite six years and were willing to go to the theatre and stayed until the show ended past midnight. Your aunt Yu (Peiyu) told us that, at the theatre, you spoke to English soldiers. When she asked you how you knew them, you answered that they were sailors on the same ship. Your boldness and lively behaviour were loveable but made us worry that you would not be easy to bring up. You have a talent for languages. You had only gone to school for half a year and had not been taught a word of English at home. At school, you had started by learning the alphabet and been there only a few months and what you learnt was very limited. Yet you were able to talk to the English soldiers. If you could have grown up in a well-to-do family environment with a number of good teachers to provide the courses, who knows you could have mastered several other foreign languages.

The next day in Shanghai, we received a lunch invitation from the calligrapher, Mr Li Zhongqian 李仲乾 and his wife. They were friends we met in Ipoh but had not seen for several years so it was a happy and enjoyable get-together. Because your great-grand uncle's funeral was to be held in Taizhou soon, we could not remain in Shanghai any longer but had to return to Taizhou to pay our respects. Recalling that seven years earlier when we left to go abroad, our respected elder was hale and hearty and his mind clear and controlled, and now we were unable to hear his soft voice, made us feel extremely melancholy. Inevitably this reduced the enthusiasm anticipated to return to our family. Fortunately, the fact that both your grandparents were healthy meant that our happiness at seeing them was not diminished. But, after several years apart, we found when we met that we did not know where to begin to talk, and being so happy felt something like sadness. We also had to pay formal visits to others of the older generation, one after the other.

The weather was getting cool so, although we were not staying long, we still had to prepare clothing for the autumn. There were other little things too trivial to go into details here. There were quite a few relatives in Dongtai whom we had to call on. After so many years, we had to leave several more days there in order to have a chance to call on and talk to them. Before long, our time being limited, we had to leave hastily and say our farewells to our families. On the day we left [Dongtai] early in the morning, your grand uncle [mother's uncle, her father's brother] was still asleep and we did not wake him to say goodbye. Unexpectedly, when our boat was about to leave, he had rushed to the pier but we could only look at one another in the distance. After the parting we would never see each other again.

When we returned to Taizhou, we stayed another ten days before we had to pack our belongings to prepare to leave again. Inside China, communications were really inconvenient. Although distances were not great, we had to change our means of transportation several times to reach Shanghai. This took much time and energy but there were no alternatives. Just before we left, we went to say our farewell to your grandmother, and all sorts of feelings welled up in our hearts. This trip home cost us quite a lot, but we could only spend so little time with our relatives, and we did not know when we would see each other again.

We travelled first by bus to Yangzhou and stopped by the home of the Yan family to talk with relatives. Mr Yan had a house in Yangzhou and seemed to have another business here but it was not convenient to ask about it. Your third aunt [Mrs Yan, mother's cousin] lived in Shanghai because her children were studying there. Your aunt Jingyi 静仪 had a job in the Education Department and lived in their house. We met her again and had a long talk to our heart's content till late and it was extremely satisfactory. The next day, we went from Yangzhou to Zhenjiang to catch the train to Shanghai to wait for our ship.

We had an uneventful journey back to Singapore; we caught the train to Kuala Lumpur that night, where we changed trains to travel to Ipoh. Our journey of over two months thus came to an end. We rushed about every day and did not rest, so it was fortunate that we were all healthy when we arrived back. At the Ipoh station, our former servant came to meet us. She was an honest and hard-working person, but unfortunately was rather weak in health and not really good for us to re-employ. It was disappointing to her, but we found someone else who turned out to be very suitable. This person was very good-natured and polite. Although she was vegetarian, her meat dishes were very tasty without her having to try them when cooking. She worked for us for five years and we were like family. Because her foster mother fell ill, she left to return to tend to her illness, and because war came to Malaya, she could not come back. She was the best among all the servants I had employed, and losing her was a matter of great regret to me.

Though you had not been in school for three months and returned only in time for the examinations, you managed to come within the first twenty in your class and thus could continue to the next class the next year. We were really happy because this meant you did not have to be held back a year. We were home for only eight months when, as anticipated, the Japanese invasion began on July 7, 1937. Our national leaders and the people, without fear of the sacrifices necessary, rose to defend the country. The overseas Chinese also did their utmost to support the cause. The local huaqiao leaders urgently organized Relief Funds and established a Women's Section. They had all the funds collected sent back to China to support the nation and provide emergency relief to the troops and the people. From then on, in addition to special donations, people also gave monthly donations. Although the amounts were small and quite inadequate, they demonstrated unity of purpose.

The Women's Division was led by family members of prominent Overseas Chinese. Mrs Wu and I joined them. Every week we would go to the Recreation Park to sell food and other goods that had been prepared or made and offered as our donations. Some days, several teams of us would go out to the shops and visit residences around the town to sell food coupons. Often we came across those who had little understanding or were simply miserly, and we found ourselves having doors closed against us. We just had to endure the rejections.

In these activities I made many more friends but that also added to our expenditures. Fortunately, prices were low and stable, and your father's salary gradually rose until it reached almost $200. We never dared to waste any of it, hoping to have some savings to meet unexpected needs when we might not be able to manage. Although we lived far away overseas, we were constantly anxious for the developments arising from the war at home. When the war started in Shanghai, the best troops and equipment were sent to the front. That enabled the forces to put up a fight although the loss of life was considerable. The three-month resistance really surprised the Japanese militarists. Internationally, too, attitudes towards China were changed. In order to sustain the long-term resistance strategy, the only painful alternative was to withdraw inland. By November, the capital was also lost. Fortunately, the Japanese militarists were so arrogant that they thought that our country had lost its ability to defend itself and would have to seek a peaceful negotiation. So they stopped and grandly celebrated their victory in Nanjing, not realizing that our country had long prepared for such a situation and took advantage of that to complete their full-scale preparations for a long war. It had the capital moved to Chongqing, and used Wuhan to serve as the interim administration centre for re-grouping the armed forces. It enabled them to strengthen their defences while drawing the enemy deep into the country and awaiting another opportunity to fight back. This was the only way for a country whose military was so poorly equipped.

During the years of the war, remittances from the Chinese overseas could still be sent, and letters to and from home continued to be delivered. When the situation was tense, family members moved to the countryside for safety waiting till matters were more settled before returning home. Although the conditions were grim, at least the family was safe and well.

⬦

One night, we asked the servant to take you to the recreation centre. She had not bought a ticket and asked you to sit among the audience to watch Cantonese opera. You were not willing to wait and wandered off to look for her. Not finding her, you set off to come home. Because you were still very young and never been out at night on your own, you were frightened, and when only a short distance from home, you cried for your father. We heard your cry and rushed to find out what happened. The servant looked desperately for you at the theatre and finally came home in terror and was so greatly relieved to find you safely at home. From then on, she never dared to take you out again.

In the autumn of 1938, we suddenly received a cable from Taixian to tell us that your grandmother had caught the flu. The doctor was unable to cure her and, after a few days, she died. We were extremely sad. If someone old like her had not been so upset by the sufferings of war, she might have been able to avoid getting ill and dying. Each time I think about that, it adds to the sense of loss. We were unable to return for the funeral to lessen our feelings of guilt. So we could only telegraph funds to help meet urgent needs.

We often worried if there was a world war and remittances were stopped, how the old and young in the family could survive. But we had no extra sources of funds to send more money home. As we worried about this, the Chinese government devised a monthly remittance plan. This allowed one to place the monthly remittance in the bank that could be drawn from when necessary. This way, the government could attract more overseas remittances. We were fortunate to have a relative, Ding Quqing 丁蘧卿, who worked for the 中南银行 (China and South Sea Bank) in Shanghai. We asked him to manage our remittances for us and after three years we had some savings that made us feel more secure.

Suddenly, the Japanese militarists, over-confident about their own strength, launched their invasion of Southeast Asia. On the 8th of December 1941, Penang was first to be bombed. Because forces were inadequate, Malaya did not manage to defend itself. In a very short time, many states were abandoned, and overseas letters and remittances came to a stop. After the war, when we returned to China and asked about our Shanghai bank account, we found that it had been very useful. For several years, the eight family members had drawn on it to avoid greater tribulations. Otherwise, the consequences were unthinkable.

At the English school, your schoolwork was not demanding. You did not often have any homework to do at night. You could have spent more time at home studying Chinese. But you were young and playful and, having no one to study with, found such study boring and thus your progress was slow. Fortunately, not far from home was a newly established private school that specialized in teaching Chinese to English school children. So we sent you to study there. It was a pity that the school started its classes at a rather inconvenient time. Its classes began at 1.30 pm while your school ended the day at 1.00 pm. You had to come home for lunch and then rush to the school. You studied there for several months. Then one day when cycling to school, you were knocked down by a car. A neighbour came to tell me about the accident and I was so upset I did not know what to do. We did not have a telephone so I could not tell your father. I rushed out of the house to find with great relief that you were not hurt. The driver of the car was a senior civil servant and the police who came to investigate seemed to have some private agreement with him. When the case was brought to the court, it was found that the cyclist was at fault. In fact, the drunken driver was the one to break the law. As it was, you were fined two dollars and the matter was settled. But as you were not hurt, I was truly happy and did not want to pursue the matter against the drunken driver. From then on, I did not dare to send you to that school and you lost the chance to continue with your Chinese, which was a pity.

After war broke out in China, more and more people came south to avoid the fighting. Quite a few artists and men of letters visited Ipoh, for example, Xu Beihong 徐悲鸿, Zhang Shanzi 张善子, Weng Zhanqiu 翁占秋, Zhang Dannong 张丹农, Huang Yankai 黄延凯, Zhang Siren 张斯仁, Li Xilang 李西浪, and they all became "literary friends" (wenyou 文友).

At the end of 1938, Mrs Zhou brought her five children to Ipoh, the eldest was thirteen and the youngest not yet three, to the Wu home to avoid the war. She was Mr Wu's sister and she came together with Wang Ruya 王儒雅 and together they all stayed in the Wu house. There were not enough rooms for them all. Fortunately, the bungalow had wooden flooring and in the warm tropical climate the problem could be easily solved. Everyone slept on the floor. In the Nanyang, this was common practice when families were large.

When they first arrived, Mr Zhou was still sending funds from China to help their expenses. But later when the Chinese currency dropped in value, he was no longer able to do so. The Zhou family could only depend on the brother who gave them twenty dollars a month for their use. Fortunately, prices were low and they could just manage. It was only after more than a year before Mrs Zhou could find a teaching job at the Peinan 培南Primary School. Her salary was only thirty-five dollars a month. The six of them lived on that and covered their clothing needs, barely surviving. The cruelty of wars that destroyed so many happy families was something really hateful.

We had been in Ipoh for eight years and were having more and more visitors. Our chairs were getting old and we did not have enough of them and so had to buy some new ones. What we paid for them was noted down at the prices at the time, so we know what costs were like. For example, the set of wooden table and chairs in the living room cost $50, the glass bookcase $15, the wooden double bed $16, the clothes cupboard with mirror $25, the second-hand radio $60, the old bicycle $30. This depleted all our savings. Not even two years later, because the war came, all these were stolen and lost. After that, for more than ten years, because prices of goods had risen high and we had no savings to replace them, we just used whatever old furniture was available.

In the summer of 1939, Mr Yin suggested that we organize a Sanjiang Tongxianghui (三江同乡会 Three Rivers [jiang] Provincial Association) to bring fellow-provincials of Jiangsu, Zhejiang and Jiangxi together to share our concerns. Funds were actively raised for this and on 25th December that year, the association was established. Apart from the people of the three provinces of Guangdong, Guangxi and Fujian, everyone else male or female could join as members. At the time it was established, there were only just over sixty members. The funds were limited so we rented a meeting-place close to the Recreation Park.

Ipoh was always an area where the influence of the Hakka people was strongest. Most of the key people on the boards of the Chinese schools were Hakka. School teachers from the Three Provinces (Sanjiang) did not find it easy to get into these schools and could only find jobs in schools further out in smaller towns. They could not come regularly to the Association gatherings and more members were from the business groups. After the association was established, it enabled those who have been away from China for years to naturally develop warm fellow feelings and greatly share and enjoy one another's company. The pity is, not even two years after its establishment, when the Japanese invaded, the association was closed.

At the end of 1939, the Wuhan Choral Society came south as part of the patriotic movement. The group consisted of twenty-six men and women and they sang in various cities of Singapore and the Malay states. All the money collected from ticket sales were donated to the China war effort. All their local living and other expenses were provided by various huaqiao groups. They were here for over a year and then disbanded to return home to China. Apart from providing all the expenses for their journey home, the local community also gave $500 to each of those who returned. Those who chose to remain did not receive that. During that year, the financial burden for the Chinese overseas was not light.

Two of the members were young ladies from Shanghai. Both were surnamed Chen but were not related. One was called Wei 蔚 and the other Xiaying 霞影. Mrs Wu saw them as fellow-Shanghainese and was especially close to them. They stayed at the Chinese Assembly Hall and it was only a few minutes' walk to the Wu home if they followed the railway line....

After the two Miss Chens returned to Ipoh, the four of us rarely played mahjong together. The reason was that, every weekend, Mr and Mrs Wu would tour around the neighbourhood. Occasionally, in the early evening, they would come to our home to play mahjong and do so without warning us of their visit. Suddenly our dinner for three was turned to one for four (adults) and we had to cook more food. Because we did not have a refrigerator and had to buy fresh fish and meat and vegetables each day, it was not possible to provide more food and could only do so by opening canned food and cooking some egg dishes. Until the start of the war, this happened five or six times. I could only buy more canned food so that we could provide some hospitality when it happened. We would play mahjong for long hours and did not stop till late at night.

The mahjong table was just outside your room and must have greatly affected your sleep….

On the night the war started, Mr Wu invited us to play mahjong and we played the whole day till late at night. On our way home we passed through the town and saw fully armed soldiers and guessed that war was about to begin. When we got home, we listened to the radio and heard that Penang had been bombed and the war had truly started. We suddenly realized that we had made no preparations for this. Unable to decide what to do, we walked around all night and could not sleep. The next morning, Mr Wu suggested that our two families leave together for a safer place; that way, we could look after one another. We agreed and quickly prepared to bring with us what we needed and leave our home. ""

Learning to Roam

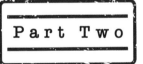

Part Two

War Comes to Malaya

WE HEARD THE echoes of war for more than four years before war reached the Malay Peninsula. After our brief visit in 1936, war started in China and the subject was never far from the conversations my parents had with their friends, and it was one of the main topics of conversation at our dinner table. Clearly, going home to China was no longer an option. With each year, the war seemed to be spreading, especially southwards towards the provinces from which most Chinese in Ipoh originated. By 1939, every day also brought news about war in Europe. Eventually, it seemed certain that war would come to Malaya. I realized it was serious when my father bought a radio so that we could listen to the news. That was exciting for me because, with my atlas, I could trace where the fighting was going on. Each time I heard a place mentioned, I would look it up in my atlas. I felt personally connected with the war-torn world and that made the wars less frightening. I still remember being struck by news of bombings in Chongqing and London occurring about the same time. That made me even more aware that the conflict was truly a world war.

I was aware of the fear that Japan would soon expand southwards after its forces took control of Guangzhou and then the island of Hainan in 1939. The British knew that the Japanese planned to use French Indo-China to attack other parts of Southeast Asia. Vichy France was helpless to stop Japan, and Britain made serious preparations to defend Malaya. At school, we were told of the Naval Base in Singapore and most of our teachers were confident that the British could keep Japanese forces at bay. After the war, when numerous books were written explaining why the British were so quickly overwhelmed, I learnt that the British feared that Japan would use Thailand to attack the northern Malay States overland, but they were better prepared for invasion by sea and had not planned well to defend the peninsula.

Japan's allies in Europe were triumphant and Nazi Germany had started their invasion of the Soviet Union. I think that most people felt that it was only a matter of time before Japan moved against Malaya. My parents, like many others, remained hopeful that Britain was strong enough in 1941 to keep the Japanese out, and I never sensed any alarm until very late in the year. In December the Japanese attacked from the north and within days, bombs fell on Ipoh. In great haste, my parents joined their friends, Mr Wu and his family, leaving the town. I learnt later that arrangements had been made for us to hide in a timber camp and rubber estate outside the town of Tanjong Tualang. The owner was the Board chairman of the local Chinese primary school who knew Mr Wu and my father and offered to help. We stayed three weeks, spending most of our time in the timber camp but moving to temporary structures deeper in the jungle when the Japanese were nearby. A few Japanese soldiers visited the camp but they were in a hurry to move on and did not harm anybody. I remember little of what we did there except that we children were excited by the experience of roaming along the edge of the jungle and learning something of the plant and animal life there. Most unforgettable for me was a severe attack of malaria, something that had been keeping me out of school off and on for months that year. The high fever that gripped me for several days alarmed my mother but, fortunately, she carried a supply of quinine and I eventually recovered.

Around New Year in 1942, we moved from the camp to a hiding-place in a cluster of limestone caves closer to Ipoh. Many families lived there and during the fortnight we spent inside the caves we saw no Japanese troops. I never knew how that refuge was arranged for our families but was fascinated by the strange shapes of the hills and the small openings that led us into caves, which to my astonishment opened onto a large clearing. The larger caves contained all kinds of little structures and we were given a couple of them to use. Somehow there was food and water and we were undisturbed, but we were also chastened to learn that people normally lived there in those unusual conditions. Although our time in the jungle and in the hills was brief and we came to no harm, it marked the start of years of semi-nomadic life. I recall being solemnly told that our two families no longer had homes to return to and that what we had with us was all we possessed.

By January 1942, the Japanese garrison in Ipoh with the help of civilian officials had restored order and basic services. Mr Wu and my father went to the town to find us new places to stay. There was no question of returning to official houses built by the government, so they looked for a place in New Town. We followed the Wu family and rented a room where all of us squeezed together on the first floor of a shop house. A Chinese medicine shop owned the building, which was on a short street just beside the new market. My parents had a bed in our small room while I slept on the floor. We were grateful to be safe. We soon heard that the Japanese had captured Singapore, and then news came that the Japanese military had killed thousands of young Chinese men in Singapore and in other places, including the Kinta area not far from Ipoh. Within Ipoh town itself, we thought it miraculous that people were largely spared. Wang Ching-wei's brother-in-law, Chan Kye Choo (Chen Jizu 陈继祖), the elder brother of his wife Chen Bijun 陈璧君, lived and worked in Ipoh, and people wondered if that made a difference.

I joined the three older Wu children in helping our families. This was a new life for us, and if we were afraid, we tried not to show it. For several weeks we set up a stall outside the market and sold sundry goods like soap and soya sauce that Mr Wu obtained for us. Then, one day, the Japanese came to the market entrance and placed several human heads on a high stand not far in front of our stall. They announced that these were heads of executed looters and warned against any kind of criminal act. We were petrified. The heads soon gathered swarms of flies and, after three days, were removed because no one could stand the stench. From that time on the market was deserted, and our parents closed the stall. The three of us then tried riding bicycles to the residential parts of the town to sell soap from door to door, but that bit of entrepreneurship was totally unsuccessful. Our parents decided to retire us, and our brief careers as salesmen ended.

Some weeks later, I had another terrifying experience when I followed some people to a small park not far from my former school on the way to the river. I wondered why a large crowd had gathered there and thought there might be some sports or a performance. We were then told it was to witness a public execution. We saw from afar a young Chinese man being led to the middle of the park and made to kneel. I still did not know what to expect. Suddenly, a Japanese officer raised his sword and cut the man's head off. The officer did not fully succeed with the first stroke and had to make a second cut before the head fell to the ground. The crowd cried out and then fell silent. The officer shouted in Japanese before ordering his men to remove the body. I was horrified and had nightmares for several nights. Although I never saw anything like that again, it made me understand how quickly people could become indifferent to acts of cruelty.

After a couple of months, my parents decided that our two families made too large a group to live comfortably together on one floor of a shop house and we set out to find another place to live. We first moved to a village outside of town where we lived with the Ho family for a few months. Then we moved back into town, this time to Old Town where we rented a room from the Hokkien Association 福建会馆. The association had a large building and ran the Peinan Primary School on its premises. This was the school where the Wu children had studied, and my father and Mr Wu knew the association leaders well. The school did not re-open after the Japanese came to Ipoh and had rooms to spare. Mr Khor, a former school principal who now worked for the Association and lived in one part of the building, knew my father and rented us one of his rooms. This was again a very small room where I slept on the floor.

The building was in an excellent location. The Wu children had told me how much they enjoyed studying in their school. The Kinta River was on one side and the padang, the best sports field in the town, was on the other. Across the padang, on a small rise, was the exclusive British club. St Michael's Institution, a Catholic school, was to the right of our building and to our left was the whole length of Belfield Street, with some of the town's best shops.

The Japanese had taken over the beautiful St Michael's building next to us to use as the headquarters of the state government. I did not know by what chance we were placed in the shadow of the new conquering authorities. One result was the whole place was well guarded, but it also meant that the few local male residents around were expected to perform neighbourhood security duties. The duties included standing at the street corner from midnight to dawn. It was done in rotation. My father did his turn a few times while we lived there and, on one occasion, when he was unwell, I took his place. I was just twelve years old but tall for my age, and with the long staff I was given to carry looked a credible guard.

My father arranged for me to be admitted to Ming Teh (Mingde) Primary School 明德小学, a few blocks away on Belfield Street, a school established by the Hakka Association 嘉应州会馆. I was put in its senior class. My teachers were Hakka and taught us in their version of Mandarin. It was a new experience and I enjoyed learning subjects like arithmetic, geography and history in Chinese instead of the classical Chinese texts that I read at home. It soon turned out, however, that not all was well. My father was troubled that the school was required to teach more Japanese when two young local teachers were sent to make us devote more time to the language. We had to sing the Japanese national anthem every morning and learned Japanese patriotic songs. My father decided that he did not want me to do that and took me out of the school. Thus began my years of un-schooling. I was a little sad to part from my newfound school friends but I soon became accustomed to finding things to do on my own and, for the next three years, did not miss school at all.

For several months, I spent many evenings joining other children running in the field. Without the British using it for their cricket and rugby matches, the field was open for all of us to play ball games, fly kites and more or less keep out of mischief. I also loved to walk on the high bund along the Kinta River, and wash my feet in the shallow river below. We lived several months with the Khors and their two sons and three daughters. They were Hokkien but could speak Mandarin. The elder son was some years older than me while the younger son was several years younger. Fortunately, the three daughters closer to my age were friendly and taught me to speak Hokkien and gave me tips as to how I could help my mother, especially shopping in the wet market for fresh vegetables and cleaning up after each meal. I confess I was not naturally filial and wished that I had a sister or two who could relieve me of these chores.

Town Boy

MY FATHER WAS worried about my education after I left Ming Teh (Mingde) School. He therefore organized a private class to teach his friends' children so that he could have me learn with them. The small class of about ten of us met three times a week, usually in the late afternoon. Here he taught us classical Chinese. My father was very keen about teaching us how to appreciate literary Chinese and learn to write it well. All of us had gone beyond the basic *Sanzijing* and *Qianziwen* and my father could assume that we knew the meaning of enough of the characters in those two texts. He first concentrated on the *Guwen Guanzhi* 古文观止, the standard collection of the most famous Chinese prose writings. He began with short vignettes by Tao Yuanming 陶渊明, like his famous Peach Blossom Land 桃花源记 and Returning Home 归去来辞, and quickly took us to the beautifully clear prose of authors like Han Yu 韩愈, Ouyang Xiu 欧阳修 and Su Shi 苏轼.

He had us memorize several key essays, and made sure that we not only understood every word in them but also mastered the rhythm and cadence of each sentence. Then he set us the task of writing this form of literary Chinese. Our private class studied together for more than a year. As we made progress, we went on to learn from other selections of prose literature. There was a lot of memory work and I remember how painful it was to write essays and letters in classical Chinese. I found essay writing a particular struggle because what we were expected to do seemed so distant and unrelated to the life around us.

Separately, my father encouraged me to practice calligraphy, something he loved to do himself, and guided me through Yanti 颜体, the style of Yan Zhenqing 颜真卿. I worked hard at my calligraphy then but sadly failed to keep practicing and never took it up again. It is the one failure in my life that I know my father keenly regretted. He also wanted me to share his interest in poetry. He began with a small number of poems from the *Shijing* (诗经 Book of Poetry), samples from the poems in *Lisao* and other examples from *Gushi shijiushou* (古诗十九首 Nineteen Ancient Poems). Finally, we went through a selection of the *Tangshi sanbaishou* (唐诗三百首 Three Hundred Tang Poems) and I enjoyed memorizing many of them. Strangely, he did not teach me to compose such poetry and never encouraged me to try. It was enough for him that I could appreciate the range and depth of feeling found among the best Chinese poets.

Years later I often wondered why, as an avowed Confucian, he did not do any close reading with me of the classic Confucian texts like the *Lunyu* (the Analects) and *Mengzi* (Works of Mencius). Of the Four Books, he only spent time on *Da Xue* (Great Learning) and *Zhongyong* (Doctrine of the Mean), taking pains to get me to understand the former thoroughly. He introduced later examples of Confucian thought indirectly through the essays of men like Han Yu 韩愈 and Ouyang Xiu 欧阳修, among others. My father never directly introduced me to the ideas of Neo-Confucian thinkers like Zhang Zai 张载, the Cheng brothers 程颢、程颐 and Zhu Xi 朱熹, only mentioning them as philosophers that I should learn from later. Maybe he thought their ideas, like their commentaries of the Analects, were too difficult for me to fully understand and did not want some of their obscurities to put me off. Perhaps he recalled the kind of classics overload that he had personally experienced and reacted against. It is also possible that the modern education theories of John Dewey that he studied in Nanjing and greatly admired taught him to give his son more space to learn things for himself.

What he did do, however, was to interest me in the prose of some leading historians and their accounts of heroes and villains in China's timeless past. He began with a few stories from the *Zuozhuan* by Zuo Qiuming 左丘明 in the *Guwen Guanzhi,* and was particularly fond of essays by Sima Qian 司马迁 and Ban Gu 班固. Later he encouraged me to read more of them from the original *Shiji* (The Records) and *Hanshu* (Records of Han). Although he merely praised the prose styles of these two famous historians, he knew that the lively stories they told captured my imagination. For example, I still vividly remember reading the biography of Xiang Yu 项羽, the great warrior who overthrew the Qin empire only to lose everything to the founder of the Han dynasty, Liu Bang 刘邦. Another memorable story arose from the letter supposed to have been written by Li Ling 李陵, the Han general who had surrendered to the Xiongnu forces after being defeated, to explain why he defected. The letter was addressed to Su Wu 苏武, the Han envoy, who had done just the opposite. Su Wu remained loyal and suffered nineteen years in exile in the northern Asian wilderness, spending many of those years herding sheep. My father may have stressed the prose skills in the essays, but they certainly stimulated an appetite for Chinese history.

He owned a set of one of the abbreviated versions of Sima Guang's *Zizhi Tongjian* (资治通鉴, Mirror for Government) that extended that great work to the Qing dynasty. He spoke to me about the contents of this work, the *Gangjian yizhilu* 纲鉴易知录 but never encouraged me to read it. He had little interest in history and probably thought an abbreviation of a classic work was not worth reading, but when I later became interested in the continuities of Chinese history, I turned to Sima Guang's work. In an indirect way, my father had prepared me to make the most of that great work when I needed to.

In these ways, my father ensured that my education continued during the Japanese occupation. Throughout those years, I spoke nothing but Mandarin and various dialects of Chinese that I was beginning to pick up. What made us different was that we normally spoke our Jiangsu version of *guoyu*, but at the time almost any variety of Mandarin was in demand.

Those learning years were not all earnest and self-improving. I remember a particular moment when I learnt something about how to teach. A rich Chinese man had invited my father to teach his young concubine to read and write Chinese. My father thought that it would be inappropriate for him to do that and declined, but the man was insistent and, in the end, my father suggested that his son might be able to take his place. The man talked to me and, as I was only twelve years old, thought I could be trusted to do that. The woman was young and pretty and keen to learn. I received advice from my father about what I should teach her and followed his instructions closely. To my surprise, I found that I enjoyed the teaching. The man was pleased to see her progress after a few months and I was paid, I thought handsomely, for my work. What

I really gained was confidence in my ability to communicate and actually teach someone how to speak *guoyu* and write simple Chinese.

In the meantime, my parents were increasingly dissatisfied with the small room where I slept on the floor and looked for somewhere else to live. There were other reasons why living in part of a public building like the Hokkien Association was troublesome and my parents was concerned not to outstay our welcome. They then learnt that a Mrs Yeh (the mother of Ye Lin-sheng 叶林生) was willing to rent us one of the rooms in her large house. She also offered to let me share a room with one of the workers in her shop. That probably clinched it for my parents. But Mrs Yeh was happy to have us because her husband, a graduate of St John's University in Shanghai, knew my father. I cannot remember how they knew each other but it was possibly because Mrs Yeh had earlier been a schoolteacher.

So we moved again, this time back to New Town. Mr Yeh was running a business and spent most of his time looking after his main company in Kuala Lumpur. He may also have thought that having us live in the house would make it safer for his wife. Mrs Yeh was very kind and thought I deserved to have a bed to sleep in. I thus had my own bed in a room with a young man who worked in her bicycle shop. Mrs Yeh and her worker spoke a dialect of Fujian province that I had never heard of. It was the Henghua 兴化 (or Putian 莆田) dialect, and very few people in Ipoh could understand it. Fortunately, they could also speak Mandarin. My roommate taught me some Henghua words and explained that their dialect fell somewhere between Hokkien and Foochow but, frankly, it was so different that the speakers of the other two could not understand Henghua.

Through my roommate, I discovered an exceptional line of business that fascinated me for a long while. He told me that Henghua speakers in Malaya specialized in the bicycle trade. He did not know how it began and why they stayed mainly in this business, but he was proud that no one else could beat them at it. This story stuck in my mind. Years later, whenever I met someone from Henghua, I asked about bicycles and that person would show a connection with the trade. Even if not directly involved, he would know a lot about it. I was therefore not surprised when a later study that was made of the bicycle industry in Malaya concluded that it was totally dominated by the Henghua. I also learnt that they did well in Indonesia as well and began to assume that was all Henghua people did. Hence my astonishment when I subsequently met successful bankers, a diplomat-scholar and a great theatre director who came from Henghua origins. And, to cap it all, I could hardly believe those who insisted that Chin Peng 陈平, the young leader of the Malayan Communist Party, was really Henghua even though he was registered as someone from a town in the neighboring Hokchia 福清 county. My stay in Mrs Yeh's house was an early lesson in the complexities of Chinese identities, a subject that endlessly challenged the Chineseness my parents taught me to accept.

I had a happy time at the Yeh house. Decades later, I met her son Ye Lin-sheng on one of my trips to Ipoh and learnt about a book that he had written about recent political developments in Malaysia, *The Chinese Dilemma* (2005). Reading that book made me realize how well the family had settled in Malaysia, and how that gave him the ability to analyze the issues that enabled the country to develop in peace. His insights into Chinese adaptations to changing national programmes helped his readers appreciate what needs to be done for a new nation-state to succeed.

One of my former schoolmates, Francis Lee, lived across the road from Mrs Yeh's house. We saw each other regularly for at least a year and became good friends. This was what I had missed living in the Green Town enclave. I never had the chance to know my classmates who lived in the town itself. The Lees were Hakka and closely associated with the mining families that supported the local Chinese High School. His father knew my father so it was easy for our families to become better acquainted. One thing that Francis and I did together was unforgettable. We joined forces to shop for fish in the market on the days when fresh fish arrived from the east coast of Malaya. It meant queuing up very early long before dawn and waiting for hours. But we turned that into fun outings and learnt to navigate the wet market so that we could get to choose the variety of fish we wanted.

What made my time with the Lee family most memorable was the way they welcomed me to join their family events. It was a large family of four girls and three boys. His mother was a handsome Hakka woman who, despite language difficulties, managed to communicate with my mother. She liked the way Francis and I got along and I was often invited to their home. I soon became fluent in Hakka and met many of their relatives and friends and even felt like a sub-member of the local Hakka community. Their warmth made my adjustment to the daily life of Ipoh town Chinese easier and I began to lose my sense of being a total outsider.

I remember 1942 as my year of adjustment. On the one hand, I felt pushed out of a self-sufficient enclosure into an open but alien marketplace. For the first time, I was living among Chinese who did not speak English but a variety of Chinese dialects and only a smattering of *guoyu*. This made me keenly aware that I had been living a sheltered life in Green Town, out of touch with the real world of entrepreneurship and hard slog. The only bits of the town that I knew before the Japanese occupation was the afternoon school I briefly attended, the bookstore my father took me to, and the cinemas that we went to a few times per year. Now we were living among the town folk as "poor cousins" who had come in from the cold, counting on goodwill and help and moving from one corner of the town to another.

At the same time, the year was also one of self-discovery and new kinds of fun. I found that I could relate to the very different peoples who lived in shop houses whose families were tied to small businesses, or those who worked for low wages and their keep but were remarkably diligent and loyal. When I stopped going to school, I saw that many of the casual friends I played with on the padang at nightfall or by the river in the morning also did not go to school, and learnt that some had never been to school at all. This made me realize that there were other norms that were very different from those I had taken for granted. Most of all, I met people who were Chinese but did not conform to the Chineseness described in the great classical writings. That opened my eyes to different kinds of plurality, to social layers and hierarchies unimaginable in the Green Town I knew. It also raised doubts in my mind about the China my parents had been preparing me for. I began to notice that, while my father was still determined to educate me in the classics, during the whole of the occupation years, my mother said nothing about eventually returning to China.

After we parted from the Wu family to live in the Old Town, my father found a little work here and there while my mother did the cooking and washing. My parents had some savings and steadily sold things that we did not need to raise money. As far as I remember, we were never desperate for cash. During the few months I spent at Mingde School, I made a few trips to the wet market to get fresh vegetables and rice. After I quit school and only studied with my father's class three days a week, I had time to wander the streets and visit the shops that were still open in the town. I was intensely curious to know what people who were unlike my family had to do to make a living.

My Cantonese improved as people patiently explained what their shops specialized in. Most sold food and groceries, or clothing and household goods, much of which they cooked or grew or made themselves. I was surprised that all the Chinese shops had altars before which incense sticks were always burning. They explained that this was done to secure protection from the gods so that their business could thrive. Some told me that their gods had accompanied them from their villages in China and connected them with others who shared the same gods. By that time, I was beginning to realize how different our family was from all of them. I asked my mother if that was because we were from another part of China. She explained that people in the Yangzi region also had their gods, and that our family's strict adherence to Confucian values created the distance between them and us.

What impressed me most were the grimy shops where men were repairing different kinds of machines or making furniture, or pots and pans and other kitchen utensils. I had never seen so many skills on display before. They had very few tools and seemed to depend mainly on their hands to shape the objects they made or repaired. I also learned how little these working people were paid. Many boys my age worked for their parents or elder brothers in their shops and received no money at all. They did not go to school and some had never been in one. In most of these families, there was no question of daughters attending school.

Many of the Chinese I met told me their families had arrived from China a few decades earlier, and that they too hoped to return to China someday, or at least to visit their families as our family had done. When I told them I had been to Shanghai, they were very impressed. Their travels would have taken them only to Hong Kong, Swatow or Amoy. After hearing that, I felt that, despite dialect differences and my family's distance from their religious and group affiliations, maybe we were not that odd. It was Green Town, the product of an expatriate system of officials which depended on having its officials stay above the crowd, that isolated us from normal living.

As the weeks went by in 1942 and we accepted that the Japanese would not voluntarily go away, I began to wonder how I could become more like the Chinese people I met daily. My parents and their friends clung to the hope that the situation we were experiencing was temporary and that the British and their allies would win the war. That was comforting. We were frightened by the Japanese soldiers in town and stayed away as far as possible from any place that they guarded. Fortunately, there were few Japanese soldiers in the town. I recall people speculating that most of the troops were fighting in Burma on their way to ridding India of British rule. Those who remained were mostly either Koreans or Taiwanese. There seemed to be an understanding that the Chinese who were prepared to be peaceful would be left alone, and that the Japanese were more suspicious of those who remained loyal to the British. In any case, the Japanese needed the Chinese to continue producing basic goods like food and tools for everybody's daily use.

No one I met in town spoke any English, and I felt totally cut off from the English-speaking part of my life. At that point, a strange twist of fate gave me a link back to my English schooling. I did not realize it at the time, but that link was to become a great help when I resumed my studies at Anderson School after the end of the war.

Another Kind of Learning

I SPENT THE first years of the occupation learning about the town and its people and weaning myself off my Green Town comfort zone. It was an eventful and ambulatory year with our family moving four times and me wandering the streets. The next two years were sedentary in comparison but two unexpected events changed the rhythm of my life, curiously both giving me a small link to the English I learnt in school before the war that I was no longer using. The first had to do with a makeshift library of English novels, the second with a secret shortwave radio I listened to in order to learn news of the war.

The Japanese authorities had been asking my father to return to his old job to help the Department of Education. My father declined but he was advised by local Chinese community leaders, including Chan Kye Choo, not to appear hostile and urged him to co-operate. He sensed a threat behind the advice, but insisted that he would not return as a school inspector but only serve in some minor position in the office. The Japanese chief education officer agreed. To my father's surprise, he was American-educated and had done a degree in English literature. When he found out that my father had a similar degree, he assigned my father to look after the large number of books that had been deposited in the department after the initial months of looting and clearing out of the homes of British businessmen, planters and officials. My father was thus re-employed almost as a caretaker for abandoned books. Once again he went to his office every morning and returned in the late afternoon. He rearranged his private Chinese class and thereafter we met in the evenings.

His new job turned out to be a great stroke of luck for me. The books, he discovered, had a painful if not tragic tale behind them. They were collected from British expatriate homes whose owners had fled the country or been caught by the Japanese and sent to prisons in Singapore. Most the books were popular fiction in English, but there were also handbooks, guidebooks and other more technical volumes. There were boxes of them, mostly unopened and it was agreed that they should become the nucleus of the department's library. My father then asked to have me brought in to place all the books on shelves and help him prepare a catalogue.

I had never before read any contemporary fiction. My father only bought scholarly texts in classical or literary Chinese and my mother was an avid reader of popular magazines; we did not have any modern Chinese novels in the house. Our books in English were the classics of literature: Chaucer, Shakespeare, Milton, the romantic poets, and a few novels by Defoe, Swift, Fielding and Dickens. Although my father subscribed to literary magazines, he never bought any works of fiction by writers who lived after Dickens.

When I unpacked the books, I realized that this was a treasure trove of the most popular English reading of the time. I quickly saw which were the most popular by the number of titles represented. The obvious ones were Agatha Christie, P.G. Wodehouse, Edgar Wallace and Edgar Rice Burroughs. I grew so fond of the Belgian detective, Hercule Poirot, I think I read most of the Christie novels in the collection. Wodehouse was initially harder to understand, but I eventually took a liking to the very English mindsets that he so vividly captured in words. Wallace gave me a morbid taste in thrillers while Rice Burroughs not only reminded me of the Tarzan films I saw before the war but also took me to Mars and the imaginary access to outer space, ultimately to the science fiction that I was later to read.

Others that attracted me were works by H. Rider Haggard and Leslie Charteris. Haggard's *King Solomon's Mines* developed a fascination for a romantic and distant sub-Saharan Africa that stayed with me for decades. Charteris contributed to my education in yet another way. His many stories based on the adventures of The Saint were quite forgettable, but he used long and unusual words on every page of his books and they taught me to use the dictionary efficiently and, in the end, greatly increased my vocabulary. Many years later, I learned that he was born in Singapore of a Chinese physician-father and an English mother, and that his father had helped Sun Yat-sen when he visited the colony in 1900. After the war, one of his nephews was a fellow student at the University of Malaya, and he told me that Charteris' younger brother was a well-respected Anglican priest who later settled in Singapore. That piqued my interest in another direction when, later in life, I studied the early history of the overseas Chinese and became intrigued by the cosmopolitan progeny of Chinese Eurasians in and outside Hong Kong.

In addition, the collection included many classic novels that I had heard of but never seen. These included novels by Austen, the Bronte sisters, Dickens, Thackeray and George Eliot written in the 19th century, and two of the 20th century, Conrad and Hardy. I also found European classics in translation by Victor Hugo, Alexandre Dumas and Leo Tolstoy. After reading the pulp fiction, which I enjoyed, I became confident enough to read a few of them in full, including *Pride and Prejudice*, *Wuthering Heights*, *Great Expectations* and *A Tale of Two Cities*. They demanded close attention. I dipped into some of the others and regret I did not read more of them before the war ended.

My father was responsible for the library till the end of 1944. He asked that I be permitted to borrow the books that I wanted to read. I started by taking home two books each week and naturally began with popular novels. It was slow going to begin with, but as I increased my vocabulary and familiarized myself with colloquial English, I read more quickly. I would read in the evening and could finish a novel in three or four days. After a while, I was reading three or four novels per week. Occasionally, I interspersed the popular ones with a few classics, but I found the thrillers and the detective and science fiction novels much more enjoyable. I cannot remember how many I read during that year but my English improved immeasurably during that time.

This turned out to be a fruitful period in my informal education. I continued with my Chinese studies. My father introduced our class to more key poems of ancient China and taught us to compare them with the great Tang poems we learnt earlier. I am not sure how many of us appreciated the finer points my father drew to our attention, but we memorized quite a few of the poems. In addition, he began to focus more on classical Chinese essays that gave us insights into philosophy and history, for example, key passages from the Confucian Analects and the Works of Mencius, and from the Chronicles of the Spring and Autumn Period (mainly Zuo Qiuming 左丘明's interpretations) and also more chapters from the two great works of history, the Historical Records and the History of the Han dynasty. My father was confident that studying these texts did us good and was optimistic that one day they would help us learn to write in classical Chinese. I cannot say that I fully understood these writings at the time, but there is little doubt that this early introduction helped me cope with my university courses when I eventually had the chance to study in China. And when I started research on the early history of the Nanhai trade in 1954 at the University of Malaya, this background enabled me to write my thesis on my own without any expert supervision.

However, my English fiction reading was a real bonus. During the three and a half years when I had no contact with anyone who spoke and read English, the novels provided a lifeline to an enriched vocabulary. My father had kept his English dictionary with him and I used it to look up every word that I did not know. I made lists each day, rather like the lists from my schoolboy atlas, and increased my understanding of the language in ways that surprised my father. By the end of 1944 when my father resigned from the Education Department to become the family tutor to a Hakka tin mining family, I was confident of my ability to read anything in English and continued to look out for books to read. I even became bold enough to think that I could write my own pulp fiction, if only to practice my English.

In 1945 I used the plot of one of the Sino-Japanese films allowed to be shown in Ipoh the year before, a fluffy romantic musical from Shanghai, as the basis for a Malayan love story. I had by then made long lists of new and untried words and thought it was time for me to attempt to do some writing. For several months, I wrote a few pages each day using as many as possible of the new words that I had in my lists. I got as far as some 200 pages when the war ended. I did not think much of the story and, once I was set to go back to school, I abandoned this first effort at creative writing and later, possibly when preparing to leave for China, lost the manuscript.

The year I spent with the borrowed books not only kept me off the streets but also gave me a new sense of freedom. I think it was during that time that I began to understand that, as long as I could read and use my mind to think, I could adapt to any condition however different. I felt I had found a purpose in life and no longer wanted to join the other children in town and be part of their community. I realized that I much preferred to be among the books that opened my eyes to other worlds, not only those about ancient Chinese beauties, poets and moralists, but also those about space travel, tragic heroes, worldly detectives, pompous fools and even honourable thieves.

In 1945, my father was employed as a tutor to the family of a Hakka tin miner who was eager to learn to speak *guoyu* and have his children learn Chinese. For this job, we moved to live in the family's house on the southern edge of New Town by the Kinta River. Our move from Mrs Yeh's to Mr Chung Sam 鍾森's house was our last before the end of the war. We lived there till the end of the year and all that time we felt secure and comfortable. Mr Chung came from Meixian 梅县 in Guangdong province to Malaya with skills in handling the electrical machinery used in tin mines. During the occupation, he bought a few mines that had become unprofitable and by revitalizing them became quite wealthy. He offered my parents a comfortable room in the main part of his house, while I shared a room in the extension at the back with one of his electricians. By that time, I had learnt a fair bit of Hakka with Francis Lee's family and could converse with the Chung family. He appreciated that but asked his family to speak only Mandarin with me. Unlike my father, he was very keen on regular exercise and got us to join him and his son in calisthenics on the lawn every morning. That came at the right time for me. I was eating well and my thin gangly body needed the workouts to fill me out. I also believe that it made me stronger and contributed to my ability to take part in sports when I went back to school after the war.

Then came another unexpected chance to be exposed again to the English language. This time, however, it was not in books but in the air. Mr Chung found out that what I had was a rare skill in his community. My English was good by the standards of the time. He had earlier asked one of his workers, an electrician, to build a secret shortwave radio in order to find out what was happening in the outside world. He now asked me to listen to the English news on the radio every morning and tell him over breakfast the main points about how the war was going. This was in early 1945.

The radio signals were not very strong and it took a while for me to get used to follow the spoken English. Most of the topics in the news were also new to me and there was a great deal I needed to learn. It took several weeks listening before I felt I could really follow what was happening in our part of the world and had something interesting to tell Mr Chung. Fortunately, he was very patient and encouraged me to keep trying until I was sure that there was important news for him. Gradually, I came to understand different kinds of spoken English, not only different from what I had learnt in school and not heard for years but also from what I thought were normal colloquial language in the novels that I had read. I concentrated on listening every morning to broadcasts in standard English. These came mainly from New Delhi or Colombo. I noted that, every now and then, they were interspersed with comments with American or Australian accents, and I soon learnt to differentiate between them. In this way, I was vicariously active in an adults' war.

I heard that the Chinese had not done well in the war ever since the late 1944 Japanese offensive in Hunan and Guangxi in Central South China, and that the British were still finding it difficult to push the Japanese out of Burma. However, it also became clear that the war was going well for the Allies at sea, and that the Americans were winning in the Pacific. By this time, economic conditions in Ipoh were worsening and inflation made life increasingly hard for everyone. But there was increasing optimism that the Japanese would lose the war and the British would return. As a businessman, Mr Chung needed to be certain what was happening. By the middle of 1945, he was asking me to listen each day for news about the future of the local "banana" currency that the Japanese had introduced. If that was to become worthless, he should buy as many Malayan/Straits dollars as he could and as soon as possible. This was also in the minds of others and, while some were ready to gamble on the value of the "banana" notes, the dollar became more expensive to buy on the black market every day.

We had been warned that it was very dangerous to operate a secret radio. The Japanese were known to have executed those whom they caught doing that, but our radio was small and easy to hide, and we used it with little fear of discovery. I felt important during those months, especially when I was able to pick up messages suggesting that the British would not recognize the Japanese currency in circulation. When I passed this news to Mr Chung, he was most pleased because it confirmed what he believed. He had been buying dollars systematically and I assume that that helped him protect his assets after the war.

Listening to the radio under such circumstances was an extraordinary experience for a fourteen year old. I was introduced to world events in faraway places that I could locate in my mind thanks to the atlas I had pored over three years earlier. In particular, battle zones in northern Burma and eastern India became familiar and I also recognized the names of some Pacific islands and Australian ports. Not least, the names of the war leaders mentioned every day were one by one imprinted in my mind, from Churchill and Roosevelt to Hitler and Stalin, from Chiang Kai-shek and Mao Zedong to General Tojo and Admiral Yamamoto. These names were accompanied by succinct comments that purported to describe each man's chief characteristics. I knew I was being provided with a somewhat biased political education but it nevertheless made me feel that our little town was directly engaged with powerful historical forces.

War not only became real; the battles described in the broadcasts both in Europe and Asia also sounded as if they were all exciting and decisive. I cannot remember most of the places mentioned but two in the Pacific, I have no idea why, stuck in my mind. They were Guadalcanal and Midway. Together with Pearl Harbour, a name that I had picked up earlier, these were names associated with spectacular American air and naval battles. I thus came to believe that the US Marines were at the forefront of the efforts to defeat the Japanese and that was why the Allies were winning. Thus my hopes for "our side" grew each time I switched the radio on.

—◇◇◇◇◇—

Those mentions of heroic victories, taken together with the popular fiction I had been reading, would later lead me up a strange alleyway. When the war ended, I discovered the cinema. The backlog of American films made in Hollywood during the war that poured into the town's five cinemas became a feast of flashing images. In comparison, few films came from wartime China and England because their film industries needed time to recover. The hundreds of films that came from the US were attractively presented, and some of them linked up with the English novels I had read. The way they captured my imagination reflected parts of the fantasy world in my mind, in which popular fiction was connected to clandestine radio broadcasts about real people at war. I became obsessed with this private world, and during the twenty months between the Japanese surrender in 1945 and our departure for China in 1947, I set out to see as many of the new films as possible. Looking back, it seems incredible that I managed to see some over 400 films in that time, most of them in English and most of them entirely forgettable.

An endless number of films could be shown because most of them did not stay for more than two days, each usually with a matinee and two evening shows per day. The popular ones were shown during the weekend and attracted large crowds. The others often played to empty houses with me one of the few in the audience. The first films to arrive were a selection of memorable films made in 1941 and earlier. Many were good and drew me to see more. Then came the flood of those made between 1940 and 1946. Some aimed to entertain American troops or to assure them of national support, while others depicted the harsh life on battlefields, at sea or in the air, and sought to assure those at home that America and its allies were doing well. Despite the fact that most were propagandistic and barely credible, I went to see them like someone who had spent three years in the desert and just found fresh water.

I never understood what brought about this obsession. It could be that the last year of the war coincided with my most impressionable age, a time when I had been reading fiction from the library and listening to triumphant broadcasts with a secret radio. With one following the other and each having an impact on my daily life, the two strands had somehow come together in a mixed English world that was entirely my own. It seemed to act as a counterweight for the time I spent in my father's very demanding Chinese class. One was on the whole pleasurable and stimulating while the other invariably called for sober expressions of duty. When peace finally came, the pleasurable portion seemed to have won out. I was not aware how constricted life had become during the three years past and was unprepared to deal with the accumulated sense of deprivation. Going back to Anderson School in September 1945 seemed not to have been enough to satisfy my wants. I was reminded, and accepted, that we would soon be returning to China. But the darkened theatre halls continued to beckon me to enter, as if to say that I should make the most of their projections of the imaginary before I faced another set of unknowns and uncertainties.

In late 1945, when things seemed almost normal, it made sense that I wanted to see what were advertised as the best films produced during the war. Having heard about them for months, I was eager to see the actions in which US Marines defeated the Japanese in the Pacific, and the battle sites of Guadalcanal, Wake and Midway. Several films referred to the drama that followed the attack on Pearl Harbour and others showed American planes setting out to attack Japan. Then there was the war fought in Europe and the defeat of Nazi Germany and the impact of that war on British cities and American families. I was particularly struck by the portrayals of people's reactions to the high price that everyone had paid to ensure the final victory.

Even more memorable were films drawn from novels by authors I knew. I still remember the moment when I realized that the film, "And Then There Were None" was based on a work by Agatha Christie that I had enjoyed reading a year earlier. Then there were the Tarzan films, that took plots from the works of Edgar Rice Burroughs, and those from the Saint novels by Leslie Charteris, and others based on works by Ernest Hemingway, Graham Greene, Noel Coward and George Bernard Shaw. I was frankly thrilled. There was no question that the climax for me was when I went to see Shakespeare's "Henry V" and Charlotte Bronte's "Jane Eyre" on the screen. I was older now and more ready to appreciate these films than when I saw the Dickens and Robert Louis Stevenson adaptations before the war.

What surprised me was how much I was interested in the quality of the films, in the acting and the directing. Thus my obsession grew and the urge to try and see every film that came to town became hard to resist. I began to make lists again, listing the films, the main casts, even the studios that made the films. It was also a kind of addiction. Although cinema ticket prices were very low, it still cost a lot to see several films each week. I neglected my studies and offered to do odd jobs to earn more money so that I would not miss the films I simply had to see. It was a wonder that I managed to take part in sports and athletic activities in school and pass my final school examinations.

—◦◊◦—

The three and a half years of the occupation changed my life. I stayed in four places, and lived in both parts of Ipoh Town. After years of waiting to return to China and being only minimally connected with the rest of the Chinese community. During that period I interacted with a range of families with very different backgrounds: the Hokkien Khor family, the Henghua Mrs Yeh and the Hakka Lee and Chung families. I also discovered that everywhere there were people who could speak some variety of Malaya's two lingua franca, Cantonese and pasar Malay. And, remarkably, all that time, while I heard no English spoken in town and did not speak it with anyone, I read more books in English than I had while attending Anderson School and, through the radio, heard varieties of English I had not encountered before. I met no Malays in the streets and only saw them when I passed their kampongs on the edge of town, and I only encountered Indians when we lived at Mrs Yeh's house. At the top of the same road, I had mixed with Indian workers on the days when toddy was sold and sometimes drank with them. I had tasted alcohol before the war, mostly during Chinese New Year festivities in the form of fermented rice that produced something that could be compared with wine. But toddy, a drink that sometimes left Indian workers reeling in the streets, was my first experience of strong liquor.

For the most part, though, I only met and talked with other Chinese during the whole occupation period. My Cantonese improved and I learnt enough Hakka to converse easily with Hakka friends. My Hokkien was inferior and the version I spoke was the Penang variety, which native speakers considered to have been corrupted. As for Japanese, I had three months of daily language classes in Ming Teh (Mingde) Primary School and learned their war songs, some of which I can still recognize. But I never talked with any Japanese and only heard Japanese spoken in the few Japanese film I went to see. A few other films were shown during the three years, including some Chinese films made in occupied Shanghai. The three I enjoyed were the film The Opium War (Wanshi liufang 万世流芳) where the British were clearly the baddies, the cartoon film based on the popular story of Iron-fan Princess from Xiyouji (西游记 Journey to the West) and a musical entitled Wanzi qianhong 万紫千红, with a very young and beautiful Li Lihua 李丽华 singing. For an adolescent, the joyous musical made a deep impression and I used its thin plot in the novel that I later tried to write.

This was a time of growing up that negated the colonial education that I had so far received. At the same time, it was also one that fragmented the classical language world that my father had wanted me to appreciate. Those years without schooling opened me to different kinds of learning. Although I was confined to a small Chinese town and had no facilities for study, I enjoyed the freedom to observe and socialize that taught me new things about people and places. I saw that it was possible to belong to no formal group or institution and still pursue some of the things I was curious about. The mental habits that I developed while roaming aimlessly around the town remained a handicap for years. It was not until long afterwards that I realized that my experiences included some sort of self-discovery. The most notable was the recognition that I was not inclined to pursue theories and abstract ideas but preferred to deal with personal dispositions and social phenomena. I was not conscious of this when the war ended and I went back to finish school, but the way I pursued education afterwards probably owed a great deal to those years of unfocused learning.

A New Norm

I HAD MIXED feelings about going back to school in September 1945. Although the British returned, nothing was really the same again. Community relations were at their worst during the handover interval, with inter-racial revenge killings occurring in several places in Malaya. Ipoh was lucky where that was concerned, but the lack of respect for the British in the town was manifest and there was a distinct loss of colonial authority. The state government under British Military Administration (BMA) called on former officials, except those who had clearly sided with the Japanese against them, to return to their jobs. Students at all the schools were asked to register for the classes that they would have gone to in 1942 had the war not broken out. Teachers were welcomed back and helped assess where to place each student following years in Japanese schools or, like me, without any formal schooling. Places in the English and Chinese schools in particular were in great demand.

The official position was to put aside what happened since December 1941 as much as possible and try to rebuild on what had been there before. But most of us knew that was unrealistic. Some of our schoolmates had fought with Force 136 on the side of the British and the MPAJA (Malayan Peoples' Anti-Japanese Army organized by the Malayan Communist Party) while others had served the Japanese. We were relieved that normal teaching could begin and I fervently hoped that I would not be kept behind because I had nothing in my wartime "education" that the school could recognize. In particular, I had studied no mathematics or science that could take me beyond what I had learnt in Standard Five.

The school, however, was eager to move its students on and I had one advantage. My English, at least the reading and writing part, was surprisingly good. I was also lucky that the English master at the School was keen to promote me and the mathematics master was prepared to coach me if I moved up. The teachers immediately decided that I could move to Standard Seven and, when the mathematics teacher agreed to give me private tuition, they placed me one class higher, in Standard Eight. This was good for my ego, but I realized later that it had sealed my fate as far as doing science subjects was concerned. I had to strain to catch up with those subjects and never quite made up for the handicap. I liked the classes in biology but I struggled in subjects like physics and chemistry.

I also found it difficult to settle down to study again. The only subject I made every effort to spend time on was my mathematics, in part because the teacher was inspiring and made the subject interesting. As a result, I made progress and, at the end of 1945, was deemed to have caught up enough to go on to the school leaving class where we would all prepare for the Senior Cambridge Examinations. I was indeed most fortunate. I would have gone to that class in 1945 if the war had not intervened. Without any schooling for more than three years, I now found myself only one year behind where I would have been. I knuckled down to make up for lost time and paid close attention to what was required, but frankly could not muster much enthusiasm for subjects like British imperial history, physical geography and general science. Had it not been for my good results in English and mathematics, I would not have obtained my diploma and thus would not have been accepted by any university.

Two things distracted me from serious study, both in retrospect inexcusable. One was a growing curiosity about the unrest in town influenced by the anti-Japanese fighters who become trade union leaders. There had been nationalist and communist activists before the war, but the world depression and harsh government measures had weakened their organizations, with many of their leaders deported to China and India. With the war over and employers under various kinds of pressure, left-wing leaders emerged to organize, especially among the Chinese, and agitate for better working conditions. The British Military Administration was poorly equipped to deal with this matter, and there were signs of growing turmoil among workers in all areas. The fact that I had three and a half years living in the town had opened my eyes to the significance of the general unrest, and I tried to understand what was happening. As I was not well read on the subject of workers' rights, I wasted a great deal of my time following something that was well over my head.

The second reason was impossible to explain even to myself. As I mentioned in the previous chapter, Ipoh reopened its cinemas with films from England and America. After years of deprivation, I was caught up in a frenzy of indiscriminate film going, undeterred by the bad films, always hoping that the next one would be better. I am unable to pin down the source of this madness. It could have been linked to my reading of English fiction during the years 1943 and 1944 and with listening to radio news about the war. It might also have had something to do with my sense of disconnect when our move from Ipoh to China was imminent. I was unsure about what to expect in China, and the hours in dark local cinema halls provided a sort of certainty. Returning to study at Anderson School seemed peripheral to my life since I was heading for a Chinese university where everything would be different. All I would need was a good command of the English and Chinese languages and enough mathematics to start fresh in a totally different environment.

—◁◈▷—

When the war came to Malaya, the Chinese there had to face the question of what they should do. Supporters of the Guomindang could pretend that they were on the side of Wang Ching-wei, but the Japanese took no chances and adopted terror methods to cow the population into passivity if not to submission.

My father had gone to Southeast Asia because he was attracted to the cause of educating the overseas Chinese, and he worked hard to maintain standards in the Chinese schools in the state of Perak and to train new generations of teachers. He carefully avoided politics and never spoke to me about the subject. Nevertheless, it must have been very difficult for people like him during the Japanese occupation of Malaya. I know that he supported the Guomindang government in Nanjing that had put an end to the warlord era, which he hated, and he approved the nationalist resistance to Japanese efforts to break China into several different parts and place them all under their control.

When he came to work in British Malaya, he saw from afar how, even before the Nationalist regime could consolidate its rule, Japan tightened its control of Shandong province, carved out its first puppet state of Manchukuo and moved further into Mongolia and North China. Furthermore, my father was personally affected; he could not return to China in 1936 when he very much wanted to because of the imminent threat of war, and continued working in the Malay state of Perak. He was sensitive to the growing Chinese nationalist sentiments there, and was never comfortable with working for the State Education Office that monitored the school syllabus and textbooks to minimize their political content. Most of the texts used in Chinese schools were written and published in Shanghai, and the British were determined to clamp down on expressions of nationalist or anti-imperialist sentiments in local Chinese schools, the more so if anti-British stories and comments were included.

I was too young to be fully aware of what my father went through during the Japanese occupation of Malaya. I took for granted that he would not work for the Japanese and, during the first months of the occupation, wondered what he was going to do. He had some savings and took part in some small business ventures, but he was not successful in any of that. As his savings dwindled, he did some tutoring and lived thriftily.

My father took a lowly job in the Education Department to demonstrate that he was not hostile to Japan, but he continued to look for opportunities to do something else. He was fortunate to find work as resident tutor for the family of Mr Chung Sam before the war ended. All that time, he never told me how he felt. I was reminded of those occupation years when we went to Nanjing in 1947, where he talked to me about the collaborators who worked for the Wang Ching-wei regime during the war. Only then did I realize that he felt this acutely because he knew people in Malaya who had connections with Wang Ching-wei and his puppet "Guomindang". He had seen many friends compromised by their relations with the faction supporting the Wang regime, and I presume that increased his determination to have nothing to do with politics.

I have my mother in me and was always more curious about people's politics, what they believed in and what they were prepared to do. For example, I heard that three of my older schoolmates joined the British-trained Force 136 in the jungle areas not far from Ipoh. All my classmates admired their courage and were very sad to learn that our Indian schoolmate died, presumably killed in action by the Japanese. The other two survived but did not return to school after the war. One of them, the Malay, I believe became a regular soldier and rose to become an officer in the Malayan army. The other, the Chinese, was Cheong Kok Ying 张国英, the elder brother of two of my classmates. He marched with the Malayan Peoples' Anti-Japanese Army (MPAJA) units in the Victory Parade in London and went on to study engineering in the United States. His experience left him sympathetic to the Chinese cause and, after completing his research at the California Institute of Technology, he went to China to work on rocket development. In the 1950s he decided to go to China against his family's wishes, and I still recall his parents' bewilderment when he greeted them on board his ship when it docked in Singapore en route to Shanghai, but did not follow them ashore.

Afterwards, I heard news from time to time of his progress in the Chinese world of science and technology. It came as a shock when I learnt later that he had committed suicide in the late 1960s during the Cultural Revolution. The Red Guards attacked him for living a bourgeois lifestyle and enjoying his Western books and music. He was also criticized for having "overseas contacts" 海外关系, a particularly insidious accusation that implied collaboration with the enemy. It was a label that caused great misery to large numbers of those in China who had returned from overseas out of patriotism or who had relatives living abroad and tried to keep in touch with them.

I met many such overseas Chinese in Hong Kong in the 1980s, after the Deng Xiaoping reforms allowed them to leave, and they confirmed that, as people suspected of having a "collaborationist" background, they suffered years of discrimination. One group, made up of people who were born and educated in Indonesia, told me that at the peak of the terror they spoke to one another in Javanese, in part because they did not want Chinese informers to understand their complaints and criticisms and in part because that gave them comfort and a sense of their separate identity.

I also remember another Anderson School schoolmate whose life ended differently. He was Chinese and had a job in a Japanese-formed

Home Guard unit. After the war, he was accused of having collaborated with the Japanese and was killed along with many others in similar positions. I heard this together with news of racial clashes in several parts of the country where armed Chinese killed Malay policemen who had served under the Japanese and fought against the MPAJA. People at the time saw no point waiting for war crime tribunals, and few trusted the British Military Administration to bring to justice those who had committed treacherous crimes during the war.

The picture was not always clear. The Japanese had their own rationale for conquest and continually spoke about Asians joining together to drive the white man out. Some local nationalists, whether Malay or Indian, believed them and took the opportunity to prepare for their respective country's independence from colonial rule. Several young Malay men, like their counterparts in Indonesia, were sent to Japan for training. Many Indians sympathized with anti-British nationalism in India and joined the Indian National Army that Subhas Chandra Bose organized with Japanese support. Most Chinese, except perhaps some of the followers of Wang Ching-wei's "Guomindang", had no illusions about Japan's real agenda and simply kept their heads down to protect themselves and their families. Some joined the resistance and came to think of the Malayan Communist Party as the best vehicle for attaining independence for a future Malayan state.

After the war, the returning British faced two major problems that they had in the past managed to control. Workers had become increasingly hostile to their employers, especially those they thought had made money during the occupation years, and were now encouraged and supported by the communists in the MPAJA. Moreover, racial tensions had been aggravated by discriminatory Japanese policies in favour of Malay nationalists and against those suspected of loyalty to Britain and China. To allow recriminations to turn violent would have torn the country apart. Underlying both these problems was the question of collaboration, an issue that the authorities needed to handle delicately.

I had been aware during my last year in school that, during the Japanese occupation, there was nothing in Malaya comparable to Wang Ching-wei's act of treachery in China. The classmates closest to me, Ong Cheng Hui, James Muragasu, M. Coomarasamy and Aminuddin

Baki, discussed loyalty in a plural colonial society like ours and made comparisons with other colonial states in the region. The issue was complex and we agreed that it was especially so for those Chinese who were fully aware of what the Japanese had done in China. We recognized that, in contrast to their hostility towards and suspicion of the Chinese because of their anti-Japanese activities, the Japanese dealt with the other communities quite differently. They looked out for those Malays who saw no reason to be loyal to the British and offered them the prospect of someday running their own independent country. They encouraged the Malays to work with fellow nationalists in Indonesia and certainly gave the impression that Japan was determined to establish a new era for Asia where Asians instead of the white races of Europe would lead.

We could see that the British were wondering how to treat Malay leaders who had followed the Japanese as nationalists seeking the chance to have their own Malay country (Tanah Melayu). It soon became clear that many British officials wanted to assure the Malays that their sovereignty would acknowledged and their rights eventually restored. They saw that the Malay rulers also felt threatened by republican Indonesians and that the rakyat, the ordinary Malays in the kampongs, feared the economic dominance of the immigrant Chinese and Indian populations. The British needed to show that they were truly back and could help them, but it was also in British interests to do so without discriminating against the non-Malay commercial and industrial workers they had brought to Malaya.

Across the Straits of Malacca, collaboration was not an issue for nationalist leaders who had been nurtured during the Japanese occupation, and launched an independence war against the return of the Dutch. On the contrary, many of those who had been closest to the Japanese military became the new nation's heroes. Similarly, in Burma the military units trained by the Japanese to fight the British refused to accept the return of British rule and declared their intention to force the British to leave as soon as possible. As in Indonesia, some of those who had supported Japan helped establish the new national government and were hailed as patriots.

We also observed that the situation in the Philippines was much subtler. The country had been promised independence before the war broke out and a government-in-exile led by President Manuel Quezon stood on the side of the United States and its allies, but other patriots who had served the administration in Japanese-held Manila found themselves in an invidious position. When the Americans returned and speedily declared support for an independent Filipino nation, they thought it wiser not to pursue the issue of collaboration too far.

My earlier concerns about wartime collaboration had been resolved in my mind before I finished school in Ipoh. Most people seemed satisfied by the findings of the international tribunal in Tokyo, which convicted some Japanese military leaders of war crimes. For myself, I did not register much of the news that I heard about trials in China against the leaders of puppet regimes. I was therefore surprised when, on our visit to Nanjing, my father made a point of reminding me of the ongoing debate about Wang Ching-wei's guilt, and told me about the different fates of his regime's supporters. I guessed that it was his way of telling me that I was now in China and that I needed to be alert to the issues that engaged people I met.

Preparing to Go Home

MY PARENTS, FOR obvious reasons, stopped talking about going back to China during the occupation years, and as I became more at ease staying with the various Chinese families in the town, the subject also slipped my mind. Being cut off from my school and Green Town friends had enabled me to look at Ipoh with fresh eyes and find a sense of belonging there, as if my years growing up from eleven to fifteen helped me to think of being someone who could be called Ipoh Chinese. I was still very different from those who spoke Chinese dialects at home and practiced their popular Buddhist or Daoist faiths, but from what my imagination could make of the world of English fiction, I felt I knew who I was not. In that way, I was comfortable among the new friends I made in town, especially those who studied with me in my father's Chinese class.

Me, my father and mother in front of our Green Town house, on the eve of our departure to China. I would have been 16 years old, my education interrupted by the war.

The moment the war ended, I was reminded that my family and I remained an oddity, perhaps not as odd as when we lived in Green Town because I had met other Chinese who also talked about going to China, but most planned only to visit relatives, not to go back for good. When my parents reminded me that we would be leaving as soon as we could afford the fares, I did not object. I recognized that it was what we had always wanted to do and nothing now stood in our way. As any filial son would do, I girded myself for eventual departure and reviewed my years in town in that light. I was divided between a sense of loss and the excitement of facing something fresh and new. It was clear that our going home was inevitable, and I decided to tell everyone in my school of my family's plans.

Many of us had changed during the occupation years, and our experiences required many re-adjustments. The most obvious change for me was that I lost most of my cohort of the Standard Five class of 1941. I was one of the very few who moved up to Standard Eight in October 1945 and the youngest of the three who joined the School Leaving class in January 1946. As a result, most of those in my class of thirty-three boys were new to me. They had been in higher classes before the war and

Studying at home in Green Town, after the end of the war.

some were several years older, but fortunately they were always ready to offer help to me as the "baby" in the class.

My weakest subject was physics-with-chemistry. Our science teacher, Mr Jegadason, an Indian with a degree from the University of Madras, was conscientious, but our school had no laboratory facilities and we had to go to St Michael's Institution in Old Town once a week to learn to do rudimentary experiments. Our mathematics instructor, Mr Ung Khek Chow, was a brilliant teacher, but I still had to ask him for extra help to understand calculus. The only area in which I could hold my own was English literature. We had a good teacher, Mr Dempsey, who made the reading and acting out of Shakespeare's *As You Like It* a pleasure. He was less interested in the other prescribed texts for the Cambridge School Leaving Examinations, Joseph Conrad's *Nigger of the Narcissus* and Alexander Kinglake's *Eothen*. I enjoyed both books because they had me turning to the new atlas I bought to replace the one I lost during the war. It was fun looking up the exotic places those books described. They made me aware that British writers were as global as the officials and businessmen who had been exercising imperial influence in various parts of the world. Despite that, subjects like geography and history did not excite me. All I wanted to know was about what each place was best known for, not least those marked red on the map. Where history was concerned, I remember thinking that the dramatic events in Chinese history I learnt about from texts read with my father were more meaningful and memorable than the exploits of British empire-builders.

My last fifteen months in school were frantic. I had not realized how much I had missed going to school. So I wanted to be into everything. I joined the school cadet corps, and we were given wooden guns to march around the school. I tried and nearly made it onto the school team in badminton, but fared much worse in other games. I worked hard at cross-country running and was proud to come second in the finals. I succeeded in getting onto the school debating team, which won against our rivals from the King Edward VII School in Taiping. In between seeing several films each week, I also sought to follow what local workers in town were demonstrating about. On top of all that, I tried to prepare for tests in the Chinese language. That was after all a subject that I would have to sit for when I got to Nanjing. However, I did not spend enough time on

my School Certificate subjects, and was fortunate to scrape by with a low
Grade One result, just good enough to go to university.

In the midst of all that, my father asked me to do something that
deeply touched but also saddened me. He found that most of the poems
he had written over the decades had not survived the many moves we
made during the war. He decided that he should collect together the few
he still had left and have them printed. The best way to do this was to use
a Gestetner machine, and he asked me to copy his poems with a stylus
onto waxed stencils. He obviously thought my handwriting of formal
kaishu 楷书 script was presentable. I was very proud that he entrusted me
to do that and spent many hours practicing before I began. Eventually,
with painstaking care, I transcribed all his poems. He thought the results
were good enough and had the stencils printed using one of the latest
Gestetner machines in town. I cannot remember how many copies were
printed and bound, but he distributed them to his friends. He modestly
entitled the volume *Tizhai jinyugao* (惕斋烬余稿 Leftover Drafts from
a Respectful Studio), and opened it by saying that he had asked his son

My father's poetry. These poems are in his own calligraphy.

to copy them by hand to have the poems preserved. When he died, my mother had the contents printed in a volume dedicated to him and, thirty years after that, I had them reprinted in his memory. It deeply moved me to be so close to him, the closest I had ever been to his inner self. But it also saddens me to think that I did not fully appreciate the sensibility and quality in his poetry and never learnt to write the kind of classical poetry that he so loved.

⸺◇⸻◇⸺

The Perak government announced it would award back pay to most of its officials, and the money my father received early in 1946 more than covered our fares to China. However, I could only take university entrance exams in China if I had completed high school. To return to China without that qualification would mean having to go to a Chinese high school and obtaining the graduating certificate there. He thought that it was more practical for me to pass the Cambridge School Leaving first and ask the Nanjing authorities to recognize it as high school equivalent, and delayed our return to China until I received the Cambridge results. The results were published in March 1947 and I obtained a Grade One pass. He immediately booked our tickets, and in June we boarded the P & O ship "Carthage" to travel to Shanghai.

I cannot recall exactly how I felt about leaving Ipoh for places I did not know, but realize it was a mixture of acceptance and uncertainty. My mother recorded her thoughts when she was in her seventies. Although they were addressed to me, I took it that she expected me to share these thoughts with my children someday. Let me end this part of the book with my mother's words about our transition to Shanghai.

> It was a smooth journey and took us only five days to reach Shanghai. Your uncles and aunts were all at the docks to meet us. We had all been through so much since we last saw one another that, when we got together, we did not know where to begin. We could only just laugh happily. Your grand-aunt had come to Shanghai for her son's wedding and was staying

at a fine residence on Avenue Joffe and we stayed with her. Your father thought his cousin's wedding was too lavish and was unwilling to attend it. Using the excuse of having urgent matters to attend to in Nanjing, he took you with him....

I had lived in the Nanyang for a long while and my clothes were plain and old, not at all fashionable, and I had no jewellery of any kind. When I went to the wedding, I must have looked like someone from the countryside. But I went anyway, just the way I was.

That final sentiment aptly describes in a few words the way my mother was and, to me, always had been. The sentence firmly captures what returning home meant to her.

My Mother Remembers the War

" When the war began, the women and children left Ipoh to go to the neighbouring town of Papan. There we stayed at a Chinese school that was available because it was the school vacations. The place was big enough for our party of twenty-one adults and children: eight of the Wus, six of his sister's family, the three of us and the two Miss Chen, and also two servants. For a while, that was more or less safe. Each morning, Mr Wu and your father still went to work in Ipoh. After a few days, it became ever more tense. But the two Chens and Mrs Wu found Papan too isolated and, on the 15th morning, went to Ipoh to do some shopping and have a meal there. Unexpectedly, at noon, when they were eating in a restaurant, Japanese planes came on a bombing mission. The young Ms Chen almost lost her life. After this bombing, everyone began to feel that a great disaster was about to befall. The government announced that all civil servants would stop work and offered everyone a month's salary. When Mr Wu and your father went to the bank to collect their salaries, the bank was about to close and they nearly did not get their money. Although the amount was not much, the money was most useful and supported our living expenses for several months.

During the bombing, I was in Papan looking after the dozen or so children. Because there was no air raid shelter, we could only bring everyone to an isolated place to hide. It was only when the sirens told us that the raid was over that we felt some relief. From then onwards, Mr Wu and your father spent days making plans. They concluded that Papan, only eight miles from Ipoh, was too vulnerable to military action and we should therefore move somewhere else. We also heard over the radio that the Government planned to defend Singapore at all costs and we considered going there. But with so many of us, it was difficult to see how we could get there. Mr Wu advised the two Miss Chen to go to Singapore and not stay with us. The two of them had worked for a patriotic cause and if they encountered the Japanese military, they would likely be in great danger. He also advised his sister to make her own arrangements. He seemed not to take into account that Mrs Zhou had no money and knew nobody and would not know where to go. Although Mr Wu was in difficulties, the decision to leave his sister and her family out suggests that he had not thought through the consequences. I was very concerned but could do nothing to help and could only leave some of our kitchen utensils for their use.

Seeing this situation led us to be very sad. At night, I discussed the matter with your father. We had no relatives or close friends for us to turn to in Singapore. We also had limited funds. I urged your father to get further away from Ipoh with Mr Wu because I was afraid that, as civil servants (under the British), they would face difficulties (with the Japanese). I was willing to keep you with me and remain with Mrs Zhou and her family. Your father did not agree, and we cried all night and were unable to sleep. Even to this day, whenever I think about this, I still feel a great deal of pain.

The next morning, Mrs Wu saw that I was determined not to go and she also decided that she would not leave. Mrs Zhou complimented me for being brave and rational. Later, friends who did go to Singapore and then returned to Ipoh told us about their painful experiences and the many life-taking risks they had to endure.

That night, Mr Wu and your father sent the two Miss Chen to the railway station. There was only one seat left and they had to negotiate with the ticket office to enable them both to board. It was also the very last train to travel. Even if we had decided to go to Singapore, there was no means of transport. We would have waited a whole night at the station, experienced the effects of parting forever, and all for nothing. Now that we were unable to go to Singapore, we had to think of other possibilities. Mr Wu and your father pored long and hard over the map and decided that the remote town of Tanjong Tualang where no roads went was a good place to hide. They went forth to investigate.

Tanjong Tualang

While they found no signs of war there, they came across people they knew. There was the owner of the timber company who was the chairman of the local Chinese School Board, and also Mr Zeng Zhiqiang 曾志强, whose family was already there. To be able to stay with good friends made things more convenient, so we decided to move there. Unexpectedly, when we had been there for only a few hours, Japanese planes bombed the owner's house nearby and killed two people, one of his grandsons and one servant maid. This made us all the more fearful. But if we wanted to move again, there was no transport and nowhere safe to go. We could only stay on and await death or whatever fate decreed. Every night, we heard endlessly the sounds of cannons causing all of us to live in dread. This was because we were close to the Kampar district, a major strategic place that was being fought over.

About the end of the month, the whole state of Perak had fallen. The Japanese troops came to the timber camp in Tanjong Tualang. In great haste, women and children were sent into hiding in the jungle behind the camp. At the camp, Mr Wu and your father had to deal with the Japanese. Fortunately, they were not violent and asked only for male clothing. They took one of my bags with a string of old coins but took out the clothes and left them behind. So our losses were not much. But everyone was tense and anxious and decided that the place was no longer safe, and that we must go deeper into the jungle. At three in the morning that night, the whole group set out, altogether twenty-six adults and children. Mr Wu and your father stayed behind at the camp with several of you boys.

Those who headed to the jungle walked until daybreak before we reached our destination. This was primary jungle with wild animals in the vicinity. There was nothing there but scores of large logs, so we had to make do using the logs as our beds and chairs. There was no shelter, so we hurriedly collected leaves from coconut trees to tie together and used them as roof coverings. Before we were ready, heavy rain fell and there was nowhere we could hide. We were all like wet chickens. That night, we slept in the open. All around, fires were lit to keep the animals away. We also engaged several of the timber workers to stand guard against possible robbers.

Thus were we like having wolves in front and tigers behind. Through the night I looked at the moon shining in the sky above us and could not sleep. A hundred mixed feelings gathered in my mind as I wondered when we could be safe again. Worrying the whole day, I almost fell ill. Fortunately, I had made several new women friends, all schoolteachers. And there were several other female members of the Zeng family. Being together for several days, we became used to the life. The biggest lack was that there was no bathroom. To have a shower, we only had a piece of cloth as cover. Mrs Wu was suffering from piles; she had to rest in the sun and was unable to get up. You can imagine how much she had to endure. Every day, food was brought to us by you and Ti Hua and we learnt that, in the timber camp, Mr Wu did the cooking while your father washed the clothes. There was an effective division of labour while we passed these difficult days.

On the Move

We stayed in the jungle for more than ten days. When we learnt that there was robbery and looting close by, and that the robbers were cruel and ruthless and worse than the Japanese soldiers, we decided that we could not stay any longer but must move again. We heard that in the Pulai area just six miles from Ipoh, there was a small cave. On the outside, the cave entrance was small and low so that one had to bend our heads and bodies to get through. We all thought that this cave would be safer. Each of us would have a space where we could sleep on a wooden plank three or four inches from the floor. This was better than sleeping on the mud floor. Each of us would pay $15 and everything would be arranged.

We then moved from the jungle to the town of Pulai where the women and younger children all hid inside the house. Not long after, several Japanese officers came and entered the house. Hearing their footsteps from afar caused us to shrink in fear. They were about to push the doors open when fortunately Mr Wang Zhendong 王振东 spoke with them and they did not enter the building. It was a really dangerous moment. Whenever we talked about it later, we still felt the sense of fright.

Mr Wang Zhendong and Mr Chen Jizu 陈继祖 were both responsible persons of the Ipoh Security Association and the Japanese were relatively polite towards them. Although behind their backs, people called them traitors, to be fair, if anyone was arrested by the Kempeitai military police and called them for help, the two worked hard and rescued quite a few people. For example, when Mr Zhong Sen 锺森 was arrested, Mr Wang Zhendong tried his utmost to set him free by guaranteeing for him.

That night, the women and younger children were moved into the cave. Although the cave entrance was small, the cave was very large inside and a different world. There were already many people inside, so we did not feel desolate and lonely. Each day, again it was you and Ti Hua who brought food to us. Going in and out was quite difficult. If you are not careful and knock your head against the sharp stone cave ceiling, the danger was to get your head hurt and bloodied.

In times of war, conditions were terrible, and it is really hard to describe them all. We were in the cave for about a week and again heard that people around were being robbed. We discussed the circumstances and thought that staying there much longer was not a good idea. Now that the Japanese had full control of the state of Perak, there was little point in hiding. We might as well return to Ipoh and consider other possibilities. Fortunately, when we were at Tanjong Tualang, we had met Mr Zeng and learnt that there were rooms in an Insurance Company building opposite his shop where we could stay temporarily. In any case, we and Mr Wu used to live in official quarters and, not being civil servants any longer, we were no longer able to return to our homes.

Getting back to Ipoh was now the big headache. We did not have transport. How Mr Wu and his family returned I am no longer clear. Your father and you travelled in a bullock cart while I sat on the back seat of a bicycle. For more than a month, we had moved several times. That we were all safe and well may be said to be lucky indeed.

We stayed in the Insurance Company building for about two weeks. One day, Mr Ho Di'an 何迪庵 came to call on us. He had established a private school that taught classical Chinese. Your father had sometimes inspected the school and had known him for a long while. Now he offered us a place to stay in his house in Tiechuan Lu (Iron-boat Road) and the rent would only be four dollars a month. He also assured us that his place had never been visited by Japanese soldiers and thus seemed to be a safe place, so we instantly agreed and prepared to move there.

Your father went back to Green Town to visit our old home. Most of our things had been looted but some books were left, maybe because it was too much trouble to burn them all. Some English books were left. We did not dare to keep them but could not bear to destroy them so your father left them with one of our neighbours, an Indian schoolteacher. As for the old furniture still left, a bullock cart was hired to transport them to the home of Mr Ho….

We moved to Mr Ho's home where our two families got along very well. I also gained two more friends, Mrs Ho and her relative Ms Li Rongduan 李荣端. They were both friendly and warm-hearted. In those worrisome times, we would chat. This helped to relieve me of loneliness and we became good friends. Your father had nothing to do and spent time reading some old texts to while away the time. We stayed there for five uneventful months. One day, we received a letter from the Japanese military administration's Department of Education calling upon all former civil servants to report for duty. To ensure our safety, he felt he had to go and report for work but asked firmly not to be appointed to his previous position. He was willing to accept a position as a clerk. Fortunately, his wish was granted and he was paid $60 a month. His position of inspector of Chinese schools was given to Mr Lin Yingqin 林颖琴, a schoolteacher who had studied in Japan. At this moment, Mr Xu Yizhou 许亦周 came specially to invite us to stay with him at the Peinan Primary School. The room rent was $8 per month. He had two other rooms, both rented to schoolteachers, one to Mr Pan and his wife, and the other to Miss Feng. Mr Xu and his family lived downstairs. For the sake of your father's work, we moved there…..

Your father worked all day…. At night, he had to go to two homes to teach young children to augment our income. He was not paid much but it did help us a little. During the weekend, he had to spend the whole night till dawn doing neighbourhood watch duty, so you can imagine how hard it is to describe his state of mind. Although your father worked hard day and night, what he earned was barely enough for us to live on. Just when he was worrying how to go on, he bought a dollar's worth of a lottery and won the third prize of $400. This helped us through a very difficult period. All our lives, we had never won anything like a lottery.

To win one when we were so hard up was indeed a stroke of good luck. Although the amount was very small, it was a great help.

I had not seen Mrs Zhou for several months after we parted in Papan. When we moved to Peinan School, we found that she and her family lived in the branch of the school nearby. So we could meet some evenings to talk and I learnt about her experiences during the early period of the war. They had first gone with other refugees to Pusing and returned to Ipoh with their companions when things settled down. When they were in Pusing, they met a young man who became her partner in the soap business and thus earned a little profit to sustain their livelihood. During all the years of the war, she found that salaries for teachers were so low that she could not earn enough to keep her family alive. So, while she took up any teaching job she could find, she also kept up her small business that provided the family with just enough to live on. The branch school was crowded with over ten families, there was so little space and so much noise all round that it was very difficult to endure it all, but having nowhere else to live, they lived there for over two years. Finally the school wanted the place back and they had to move out of town to a remote village where pigs were being reared. Once I went to visit her there. When I saw the conditions under which they lived, I could not stop my tears. What could we do when we were ourselves in such difficulty and could do nothing to help?

For the past year, there was no school for you to attend and no books to read. You would spend the days at the Wu home doing nothing. In the spring of 1943, you began to attend Year Six at Mingde Primary School. When you finished at the end of the year, there was no school for you to go to. Not only were you without schooling, you also lacked any spiritual food so that a teenager like you was sitting there not knowing what to do. Not long after, your father was asked to look after the library in the Education Department and that was agreed. Each day, you would go with your father and there were at least some books for you to read and not waste your time.

When we were living with Mr Xu, we often felt very uncomfortable but there was nowhere suitable for us to move to. Then one day, your father met a schoolteacher whom he had known for several years. When they were chatting, he said that his hometown friend, Mrs Ye, had a house at the Tanjong Rambutan bus station that had two vacant rooms. One was rented to a tenant mother and daughter. She herself lived in the room downstairs. Because she was often travelling to other towns, she hoped to find an honest and reliable family to stay in the house. The teacher friend introduced us to Mrs Ye and she unconditionally agreed to let us move in without having to pay rent. Getting such an ideal place to live was really something most precious....

Back in New Town

After our move, our home became peaceful and comfortable. Unconsciously, our spirits rose a fair bit. Your schoolmate, Li Maoxing 李茂兴 (Francis Lee), lived across the road so you now had one more place to enjoy yourself. Twice every week, in the middle of the night, the two of you would go to the market to queue up for some very cheap fresh fish. Because we had long been deprived of the taste of fresh fish, you were prepared to sacrifice sleep but really what was gained could not make up for the loss.

As the war dragged on, the price of goods rose daily while our income was as before. It was difficult to keep life going. What we still had that we could sell was but a typewriter. A year earlier, we had thought of selling it and asked for $500. A year later when prices had become several times higher, your father still wanted $500 for it. The buyer thought that was too cheap and voluntarily raised the price to $600 and the sale was completed. But we were careful as to how we should spend the money. Just at that moment, a friend wanted to invest in padi planting. We invested the money in the hope that when the padi was harvested, we could have rice to keep us alive. Several months later, we received our share of rice.

At that point, a teacher named Zhang Ji'an 张济安 provided an introduction for your father to become the family tutor to Mr Zhong Sen. The offer was to provide us with food and accommodation and $100 for expenses. Your father discussed this with me. Moving to Mr Zhong's place would not be as comfortable as living in Mrs Ye's house. But food was the biggest problem and we did not know how long more before the war would end. Now that there is this opportunity, we should not let it pass. So we decided to accept the offer. We would now not be short of food, so we gave the rice to Mrs Zhou and packed our old furniture to move to Mr Zhong's house.

The Zhong household consisted of his mother, his wife and second wife, six children, his wife's sister and her husband and children and also a nephew. With all living under one roof, this looked quite complicated. But Mr Zhong was a strong authoritarian figure in the house and everyone was afraid of him, thus everyone lived very peacefully. When your father started teaching, Mr Zhong also studied *guoyu* (Mandarin) for about a month before he stopped. After that, your father taught Chinese to five children and found that quite boring. After about four months, we suddenly heard that two atomic bombs had been dropped on Japan and the Japanese had unconditionally surrendered. It was really cruel for the hundreds of people in the two cities who were killed or wounded. But had the war continued, there could have been even more incalculable losses of lives for the armies and peoples of many countries. Ultimately, those who started the war deserved to be punished but it was truly sad to see that so many of the innocent was also harmed.

End of the War

When the Japanese surrendered, the great joy amongst all was hard to describe. Your father returned to his original job in the Education Department. After three years and eight months, his salary increments were taken into account and rose to $250 per month. But prices had risen so high that it was really worrying. Each dollar was now only worth about ten cents at pre-war prices. Although prices did slowly come down, they were still several times what they were before the war. At the time, salaries were not yet adjusted, but the government offered forty-four months' half pay to compensate for the money's loss of value. For the civil servants, it was like winning a lottery. Your father received a total of over $5,000. We could thus use this money to make up where we did not have enough. We also immediately wrote home and remitted funds to our family and let them know that we were well.

At the time, there was a great shortage of government quarters and your father was unable to get one. So we stayed on at Mr Zhong's. There were many inconveniences living with so many other people. One day, your father went out to see his friends and did not return. Actually, he had come back and was resting in your room because he was concerned that, going upstairs so late, he would disturb all those already asleep. Although it was peacetime, security was very bad and there were often assaults and robberies, so I was terribly worried and could not sleep all night. Next morning, I went to your room and found your father sleeping in your bed. I had lost sleep for nothing.

Another time, Mr Zhong's bicycle was stolen. They misunderstood and accused you of taking it for a ride and losing it. They did not realize that, although you were very naughty, you would never take anything from others without permission. When so unjustly blamed, you were very unhappy. Without taking dinner, you went out. We realized something was amiss. After dinner, we quickly went to look for you everywhere. Late into the night, we were still unable to find you and were really worried because there was nowhere else we could look. In the end, we went to the air raid shelter and called out your name many times and you finally responded and came out. We explained and consoled you until you agreed to come home with us. All this we did not mention to anybody else. Not long afterwards, another bicycle was stolen and all was clear. Mr Zhong realized that there had been a misunderstanding about your responsibility for the first bicycle's loss and was somewhat apologetic which, coming from him, was quite a gesture.

Your father was no longer teaching the family, so we should have been paying for our food and lodgings but we thought actual cash payment would not be accepted so we bought rice, milk, cod liver oil and other food to show our appreciation. We did not expect to stay another half a year. Fortunately, we all got along quite well and it was not until March of 1946 that we moved out and, by some coincidence, returned to the quarters we had before the war.

After the war, all the schools resumed in September. You were promoted to Standard Eight. After two months, with the new school year, you were promoted again to the graduating class. Your study of mathematics and science had been disrupted and that was the reason why you did not go on later on to study science subjects at university.

About a week after the end of the war, the Sanjiang compatriots actively sought to raise funds to revive the association and asked its members to make special contributions. Even before the war's end, we had through listening secretly to the radio learnt that the Japanese "banana" currency would not be recognized. So when it was still usable, we gave what we had left to our friends. As a result, when the association asked for our contribution, we had no more money in hand. I then remembered that we had left a crate of soap with Mrs Zhou so asked her to sell it for us. She told us that she had sold it earlier when she was short of money. You can imagine how poor she was to have done that. Had I known, I should not have mentioned the matter. That incident made me feel very bad.

During the occupation years, Mr Wu went into the Western pharmaceutical business and, during the last two years of the war, did very well and had a good income…. He thought the value of the Japanese paper currency could be equivalent to the Straits dollar. We heard that he had bags of "banana" dollars. Everyone thought that they would be useless but he was confident and, after studying the matter with his friends felt that they would be worth at least half the value of Straits dollars. When the broadcasts announced that they were worthless, his son Ti Hsien quickly used the money to buy several motorcycles and old chairs, tables, beds and cupboards. The rest of the money could then be thrown away.

Had the banana money been worth half the Straits dollar, Mr Wu would have been a very rich man. All his life, he was interested in business but unfortunately he was never successful. After the war, when he received over $7,000 as his compensation, he joined with a local business leader to go into tin mining. After less than a year, the whole sum was lost. He was always so short of funds he could not support his eldest son to go to university. That was a great pity. His son was very intelligent. After teaching himself for many years, he invented a kind of chemical that enabled him to manufacture all kinds of utensils and this laid the foundations for a sound business and he is now a significant industrialist….

When Mrs Wu was six to seven months pregnant, I went to see her and saw her lying in her bed. She was bleeding a little but was not concerned. The doctor only told her to rest. Because we had no telephone, we were not able to keep in touch. Your father was away in Singapore with some of our compatriots to raise funds, so it was hard to know what was happening in their home and even harder to find out when she was due to give birth. The private doctor had advised her to go to the hospital. When she arrived at the Ipoh General Hospital entrance, she met by chance a nurse friend who said that that hospital's doctor was no good and had caused patients in his care to die. Mr Wu then drove to Batu Gajah Hospital. This brought a delay so that it was evening before they reached the hospital. Mr Wu, Ti Hua and a maid were at her side to keep her company. She was in no discomfort and, until past eleven at night, was not ready to deliver. The doctor advised Mr Wu to return to Ipoh to rest and assured them that both mother and child should be all right. They were happy to hear this and went home leaving the maid to stay with her, not aware that not long after they left, the mother began to give birth to the baby and began to bleed profusely. Shortly after that, she died. They had no telephone at home so there was no way to tell them the news.

The next morning, father and son returned bringing breakfast for her only to hear from the doctor the details of how she had died some hours before. This was a great shock and both father and son broke down in grief. But all they could do was to bring the body home for the final rituals. All this I did not know and Mrs Zhou also knew nothing. I was having breakfast with you when the terrible news reached me. I could not help being overwhelmed and burst into tears and rushed to pay my respects. To have lost her so suddenly left me in deep sadness. She and I had been friends for fifteen years and we had seen each other at least five hundred times. She was the friend whom I have been closest and most often in touch. Each time I think of her, I feel I really miss her.

In the winter of 1946, Mr Wu was promoted and transferred to the Education Department in Kuala Lumpur. Your father and he had been colleagues for more than ten years and saw each other day and night. Now that he was to be transferred, they were both very sorry to part, confirming the adage that there is no such thing as an unending banquet. ”

To Nanjing

Part Three

Extended Family

MY FATHER was in a hurry to take me to Nanjing because he did not want to attend his cousin's extravagant wedding party. We spent four days together and it was the first time I had my father largely to myself. They were important days in my life. In the next chapter, I shall use that as an introduction to my nineteen months' stay in Nanjing. Here I shall set out the background to why it meant so much for my parents to re-connect with our extended family.

After our Nanjing trip, my father and I returned to Shanghai and picked up my mother to make the journey together to our family home in Taizhou. We spent three more days in Shanghai. My father's younger brother was working there and so were several Wang cousins, including one who had married my mother's distant cousin and was thus doubly related to us. My clearest memory was of my grandaunt, my grandfather's only sister, whom my father was very fond of. My mother had stayed at her flat in Avenue Joffe. Now that the grand wedding was over, my father even took me to call on my uncle and his newly married cousin.

I had not heard much about having family in Shanghai, so it was my first taste of the wider cultural networks of leading families in Jiangsu and Zhejiang. Such networks had flourished during the Ming and Qing dynasties. Although there were many other networks throughout imperial China, literati networks were very strong in these two provinces. In our family, my grandaunt had married Xu Senyu (徐森玉, better known as Xu Hongbao 徐鸿宝 and originally from Zhejiang), a highly respected scholar and connoisseur of rare books and documents, art and antiquities. He had worked in the Qing History Archives and was director of the Peking University Library before becoming head of the ancient artifacts division of the Imperial Gugong Museum. He was known for having helped save collections of rare books and artifacts during the Sino-Japanese war.

My father was a great admirer of this uncle and very proud of him. He was less comfortable with his cousin, Xu Bojiao 徐伯郊, who had an entrepreneurial bent and was a very successful speculator in the Shanghai stock market. My father rarely showed his feelings about people he disapproved of, but he made clear to me what he thought about his cousin's lavish marriage to the daughter of a Sichuan general.

Many years later, during the Cultural Revolution in 1973, I visited the Shanghai Museum and heard that Xu Senyu had been its director before his death. The museum had not yet re-opened to the public but our group of historians from Australia received special permission to visit it. We were told of Xu Senyu's efforts to protect its precious collection through the civil war years and also that he had been asked by the retreating Nanjing government in 1949 to help move the Gugong collections to Taiwan but had refused to do so. What we were not told was that he had been punished as a "rightist" in 1958 and cruelly persecuted during the Cultural Revolution, when he was already in his late eighties. He died a bitterly disappointed man in 1971 at the age of ninety.

After the fall of the Nanjing regime, his only son, the cousin my father disapproved of, had business interests and property in Hong Kong and later moved there to re-invent himself as an art connoisseur. By the time I met him again in the 1960s, he was particularly well known for his collection of works by his friend, the painter Zhang Daqian 张大千. When I was at the University of Hong Kong in the late 1980s, I saw a part of his collection of Zhang Daqian's paintings. A catalogue that was published in Beijing in 2013, ten years after his death, attracted wide attention among Zhang Daqian's admirers.

When I first met him in Shanghai in 1947, he was basking in his success with stock market futures. When I later learnt about the inflationary conditions in China, I marvelled at his audacity, but was not surprised that his fortune came crashing down when the national economy collapsed. What intrigued me was that someone with his literati, artistic and antiquarian background could have succeeded, however briefly, as a swashbuckling entrepreneur.

After three days in Shanghai, we set forth to go home. I remember going to Zhenjiang by train and taking the ferry north across the Yangzi to Yangzhou and changing to a local barge at a place called Xiannumiao 仙女庙. I loved the name, meaning Celestial Fairy Temple (this name has now been changed to Jiangdu), my first taste of what I saw as traditional whimsy that represented an ancient faith in Daoist spirits. The barge took us through a maze of canals where everything was flat and wet, stopping at an occasional village for passengers to disembark. We stayed on board most of the way to Taizhou. When we did the last lap by bus, I understood why barge travel was preferred. The bus was packed with people and poultry and broke down several times so that, although it was only a short distance, it took us half a day to complete that last lap.

We spent a couple of weeks in Taizhou and met many relatives, but I can no longer recall the details of what we did. The two moments that stayed in my mind were seeing my grandfather again and meeting the cousins I had first met in 1936, now ten years older. I was reminded that, at that time, we played together every day. But this time our visit was too brief and, with regret, I never got to know them. Years later, I learnt that Shengwu died in Tibet and Chengwu (Anbao) was sent as an army nurse to look after the casualties of the Korean War. I met her again when she visited my uncle in Hong Kong in the 1990s and she seemed content with her life. Their younger brother, Jingwu, became a Russian language interpreter and died in Urumqi in 2001 before I could visit him. In 1947, I was introduced to the newest member of the family, our youngest cousin, Weiwu 緯武, the only child of my father's other brother, who was then only seven years old. His father was working in Shanghai while he and his sick mother lived with my grandfather. After his mother died, he joined his father in Hong Kong and then went to Taiwan, where he did national service and was briefly stationed to guard the island of Quemoy (Jinmen 金门) against communist invasion. After university studies in Taiwan, he went on to study agriculture in New Zealand and then librarianship in Australia. He is now happily settled with his children and grandchildren in Sydney.

I also met my aunt, my father's only sister, who had married into the local Pan family. In 1988, when I visited Taizhou again, I met my aunt's son, my cousin Pan Jiahan 潘家汉, who was then principal of the

Provincial Taizhou High School. This was the local school in which many members of our family had taught, and whose alumni included my father and several uncles. On my later visits, I found the town rapidly changing. I was not able to locate the site of my grandfather's own house. The original large Wang family home is now part of a Buddhist home for the aged, and the district in which it is located is totally unrecognizable.

Roots

I never thought I would one day want to search for my roots. Having been brought up with so many stories of the family, and having visited Taizhou, Nanjing and Shanghai when still at an impressionable age, I felt I knew more than enough not to have to search further. But I soon realized that I had forgotten many details and was vague even about what my mother had told me. When my wife, Margaret, told me how much she regretted not asking her mother about her family when she was alive, I thought it was time I read the Wang family biographies again. I had looked up the lives of a few of them some years ago and recall being sorry not to have seen the family's genealogy. There were many gaps in the biographies because my great-granduncle, who compiled them, selected only those who had careers that he thought worth recording. Subsequently, I found the manuscript of his genealogy in the Taizhou Municipal Library, and was astonished to learn how large the lineage was, and how many thousands of names were included.

   Our ancestors were peasant farmers from a county called Qingyuan 清源, now absorbed into Qingxu 清徐 county in the municipality of Taiyuan, the capital of Shanxi province. In 1369 two brothers were recruited to be soldiers at the beginning of the Ming dynasty. One of them served in the garrison in Zhengding in Hebei, the next province to the east, and the other in Guanhaiwei 观海卫, near the port city of Ningbo in Zhejiang province. The latter was a garrison town providing coastal defence against "Japanese" (Wako) pirates.

   Our northern branch lost touch with this Guanhaiwei (Ningbo) branch but, at the end of the 16th century, a commander in southern China named Wang Shangwen 王尚文 called on the Zhengding branch.

There is a record of the two branches being in touch for some years before once again losing touch. Local research in Guanhai now confirms that the military family there did originate from Zhengding. It turned to business ventures in the 19th century and became rich, only to lose their fortune after the communist takeover of 1949. When I visited the town in 2014, I was taken to their family home and could see that it had once been a very fine house.

Our family history confirms military service could lead to social mobility for peasant families. The branch in Ningbo stayed with the military for several generations and then became successful in business, especially after the opening of Ningbo and Shanghai during the 19th century. Our own branch in the north was less adventurous. A few individuals passed the local and imperial examinations and joined the local gentry. The option for someone who was unsuccessful in seeking upward mobility was to remain with the military or work as peasants.

Our distant relatives in Zhengding have now updated the Wang family genealogy. When I met them earlier, they were pleased to learn about the branch that migrated to Jiangsu in the 19th century and about those of us who had emigrated. They made notes about that branch and have included some details in the new genealogy. The editorial team led by Wang Wuchen 武臣 published the *Zhengding Wangshi zupu* 《正定 王氏族谱》 in December 2016. The greater part of the genealogy up to the 19th century is the same as that in the manuscript now in Taizhou Municpal Library.

From this new version, I now know that the stem branch of the family had its cemetery in Sanlitun village (三里屯村) but that was turned to farmland during the Cultural Revolution. The family's memorial arch (paifang 牌坊), which dominated the main street of East Gate suburb, was torn down around the same time.

The Wang surname is so common that it is not easy to be sure how the different Wang families are connected, even those within Zhengding county. For example, Wang Shizhen 王士珍 (1861–1930) was head of the armed forces under President Yuan Shikai and served briefly as prime minister in the warlord-dominated republic. He came from a peasant family of the village of Niujiazhuang 牛家庄 close to the city but somehow had been tutored and cared for by our East Gate 东门 Wang family. He joined the army, did well during the war in Korea in the 1880s and was put in charge of military training, eventually rising to the highest ranks of the Qing forces. Despite his record of aiding the warlords, he is remembered positively as a local boy who made good. Today, he is depicted as having scholarly interests, and the large home he built has been restored. Because he had grown up with our Dongmen stem family, our genealogists were curious to know if he was a distant relative but have ascertained that he was not of our Wang clan.

—◁◇◈◇▷—

Our founding ancestor in Zhengding prospered, and one branch of the family broke through the social barrier in the 16th century, producing its first *jinshi* graduates and joining the literati. That branch established its main family home in the Dongmen (East Gate) district within the city walls of Zhengding town. The Wangs flourished till the end of the Ming (1368–1644) and seemed to have kept their heads down during the early Manchu Qing dynasty. By the 18th century, however, they were producing examination graduates again, and they remained prominent in the early and mid-19th century, with Wang Dingzhu 王定柱 (1761–1830) holding high office in the distant provinces of Yunnan and Sichuan and then in Zhejiang. His sons later served as officials in Jiangsu, and two of his grandsons moved their families there permanently.

They were Wang Yinhu 王荫祜 (1824–75), my great-great grand-father, and his elder brother Wang Yinfu 王荫福 (1822–81), who moved to Taizhou in 1869, after the end of the disastrous Taiping rebellion of 1851–64. This period marked the beginning of hard times for Qing China, a decade after the Treaty of Peking. From then on, our branch should really have been identified with Taizhou but Taizhou had other long-settled Wang families, including one that produced the great Ming philosopher and activist, Wang Gen (王艮), so our family was always known as migrants from Zhengding in the north. When I went to Zhengding in 1983 to learn about my ancestral home, I met Wang Wuxiong 王武雄, the head of the clan there, whose *wu* generational name made him a very distant "cousin". My own Wang branch remained in Taizhou during the first half of the 20th century, but many of the younger members have dispersed because their jobs took them elsewhere in China, and very few are left in Taizhou.

Wang Yinhu's eldest son was a prolific writer, Wang Gengxin 王耕心, the elder brother of my great-grandfather. He updated our family genealogy and his draft has survived. The Taizhou Municipal Library made a copy for me in 2014. I do not know whether he meant to have the genealogy printed. He had updated it to include his children's generation but the work was unfinished when he died in the early 1900s. He did complete a volume of family biographies, the *Zhengding Wangshi Jiazhuan* 正定王氏家传, and published it in 1893. All members of the clan received a copy of this work. My father showed me his when I was a schoolboy in Malaya. He took it with him when he moved from city to city and it stayed with me after he died. When I met members of the family in Zhengding, I was happy to see that their copy survived the Cultural Revolution, quite unusual when all families were asked to destroy their genealogies. Other copies now appear in library catalogues in China, Japan, Europe and the United States.

As my mother put it, the Wang family was very orthodox and remained loyal to the Qing dynasty during the period of China's decline in the 19th century. The grand uncle my father liked very much, Wang Leixia, served as head of several educational institutions in Nanjing, including one that educated the children of Manchu noblemen in the city. His son was a member of the Constitutional Government Promotion Society, which was founded by some of the highest courtiers and supported by several Manchu princes. From the family biographies, there was no sign that anyone was aware of the impending end of the dynasty, and of the literati as a social class.

In many ways, our family was typical of those who were not directly involved in the political issues of regime change. For example, I have found no evidence that any of its members engaged in debates about the grim fact that the Western Powers defeated the Qing Empire and were penetrating deep into the Chinese interior. Instead, Wang Gengxin's generation, as well as his sons and nephews (including my grandfather), remained devoted to Confucian learning and served as teachers and college heads. Many of them, after retirement from public office, became keen supporters of Buddhist revival activities. The original family home in Penglaixiang 蓬莱巷 eventually became a Lay Buddhist Home. When I first visited Zhengding, I noted with interest that the main branch of the clan there lived on the same street as one of the historic temples in northern China, the Longxing Temple (隆兴寺, originally called the Hidden Dragon Temple). The Wangs I met confirmed that the family had always been supporters of that temple.

Some published writings of the three generations from Wang Dingzhu survive, but they are very rare, and none deals with issues of contemporary concern. A few works also survive in manuscript form in the Taizhou library. During my visit in 1947, however, the family said nothing of these conventional writings. Neither did the family appear active in the nationalist cause or sympathetic with the left-wing opposition. My mother ventured the opinion that my grandfather disapproved of Sun Yat-sen and his followers because he held them responsible for the destruction of the imperial Confucian heritage. If correct, this attitude illustrates the conservative family position towards the idea of modernization.

My grandmother died during the Sino-Japanese war. I recall her gentle face when I first saw her in 1936. She was from the Chen family in Taizhou, but her family had, like my mother's in Dongtai, migrated from the historic port-city of Zhenjiang. My grandmother was the daughter of Chen Tingzhuo 陈廷焯 (1853–92), the author of a volume of *ci*-poetry criticism that was published after his death in 1894. That work was later considered a major contribution to the study of *ci*-poetry, but the members of the Wang family I met showed no interest in poetry and literature. I wondered why my father was different, and when I eventually read Chen Tingzhuo's writings, I realized that my father's love of literature might have come from his admiration for his maternal grandfather.

Family

When I saw my grandfather again, I found him in good health. He was stoic and undemonstrative but we knew how pleased he was to see us. My father was understandably emotional, especially about not having been around when his mother died. With his father, he was formal and respectful as was expected of a filial son, especially one who had been away for so long. They spoke privately on several occasions and I only picked up a little from my mother about what they discussed. Some of it had to do with property and ancestral lands lost during the many wars that their part of the province had gone through. I also understood that the countryside was in the hands of armed units of the New Fourth Army that sided with the communists. I cannot remember visiting my grandmother's grave; we might not have gone for reasons of safety. The ancestral rituals were conducted at home in the presence of our relatives.

My father talked often with his youngest brother. There had been a brother in between who, when he and his wife died, had left two sons and a daughter to be brought up by my grandfather. My young uncle, like my father, also left home to work to help support the family, in his case, in Hong Kong where he lived after getting married. When the war came to Hong Kong, he and his wife and son escaped into the interior and spent most of the war in Guangxi and Hunan. After the war, he worked in Shanghai and sent money to his wife and son in Taizhou to support the household. Money my father sent from Malaya after the war ended also helped the Taizhou family. Altogether, times had been hard. Fortunately, their sister, my aunt, was around.

My aunt married into the Pan family. Her husband was my father's schoolmate and went on to graduate from Jinling University in Nanjing. He taught mathematics at the school where three generations of the Wang family, including my father, had taught. He was highly respected and was briefly acting principal of the school. The Pan family was a deeply rooted local family and assisted the Wangs whenever necessary. This made my grandfather's life, with three grandchildren in his care, bearable through the worst days of the war, when his two surviving sons were far away. At the time of our visit, Mr Pan was still teaching at the same school. His son, a graduate in physics from Peking University, later became the school's headmaster. In 2002, local pride reached a high point when an alumnus of the school, Hu Jintao, became secretary-general of the Communist Party and president of China and a new history of the school was produced. In it were the names of those of our family who had either taught or studied there. I saw a mistake they made with my father's name, and they promised to have it corrected.

I cannot recall how many members of our family were in Taizhou when we got there in 1947. I remember meeting grandaunts, uncles and cousins and have a photo that shows my grandfather, our family of three and my uncle's family of three, my aunt and three other cousins who were my father's second brother's children, plus one granduncle who was my grandfather's first cousin.

With our Taizhou relations. My grandfather in dark jacket and with a beard, sitting down with my "13th grandfather".

The granduncle in our photo is interesting. I called him, according to family tradition, "thirteenth grandfather". As my mother explained, there were fourteen males born in my grandfather's generation; my grandfather was the third of them and I had in theory thirteen granduncles. I cannot recall how many of the fourteen survived, but my mother said it was common for male babies not to survive. My grandfather's two brothers had died years ago and they left him only one nephew, a young man I had met in Shanghai where he was studying hydraulic engineering in Jiaotong University. Of my grandfather's several cousins, two were especially close to him. They were numbers ten and thirteen, and were brothers. Number thirteen was a teacher at the local school, and I had met his daughter, an only child, in Shanghai. Coincidentally, she was married to a Ding who was the grandson of one of my mother's numerous "cousins", so we were doubly related. It was another example of how notable families of the province were locked in extended relationships.

My granduncle number ten, who had died several years earlier, was the first in the family to study abroad in Japan. His father, Wang Leixia, was appointed to the Chinese embassy in Japan to take charge of Chinese students in 1901, and he went along. He later graduated with a degree in biology and taught in various institutions, most notably in the Wuchang Senior College in 1913. Wang Leixia was admired as a learned teacher who headed several institutions before the fall of the Qing dynasty. He taught my father the Confucian classics and was the calligrapher my father emulated when practicing his calligraphy.

This tenth granduncle's widow was not in the photo. When I met her later, she told me about her two older sons (my uncles) and daughter (my aunt) who were all studying abroad. The three were graduates of the university I wanted to get into, The National Central University, so I was very keen to hear about their progress. In 1947, her sons were in America. The elder, Luowen 雒文, was a chemistry scholar who worked on beet sugar, while his brother, Yawen 雅文, was a mechanical engineer who specialized in automobiles. Her daughter, Hengwen 蘅文, followed her father in studying the biological sciences and, after graduating from medical school, was doing research in cell biology at the University of Zurich. All three chose to return to China after the communist takeover and suffered during the Cultural Revolution for having foreign connections. Fortunately, with Deng Xiaoping's reforms, they were reinstated in their jobs and the chemistry professor eventually became president of the Changchun Institute of Technology. His sister worked as a researcher in Shanghai and made her name in the field of physiopathology and published books on experimental oncology and the relations between cancer and the environment.

I got to know the engineer brother best. By the time I met him in 1980, he had retired to enable his son to get a job in his factory. As a result, he did not benefit from the rise of the car industry in the 1980s, and he regretted retiring early because his son made little progress at work. His daughters fared better. One became a professional accountant. Another was scholarly and became a history professor at Nankai University specializing in collating and annotating Ming and Qing editions of rare texts.

The Wang family has spread out to different parts of the world. Most are now losing their links with their families in China. What is interesting is that members of the stem family in Zhengding have been trying to track their connections, and place them on record within China. How much difference that will make to the clan I do not know, but it is one example of the way many people across China and many clans abroad are trying to keep linkages alive. I expect these efforts will go on contributing to the national enterprise of reviving traditional Chinese family values, seen as one of the key steps in restoring Chinese culture to its original distinctiveness.

Getting to Nanjing

NANJING WAS NOT China, nor was it our home. But it was where my father found work and where I hoped to get into university. It seemed natural for us to visit the city almost as soon as we stepped on Chinese soil. Thus our first visit was especially memorable. Another reason I remember my first visit there is that it was the first, and only, time when my father and I were alone and talked about modern China and matters not related to literature or Confucian thought. He took me to places that left me with many questions that remained unanswered for many years. Long afterwards, an event or something I read about would lead me to recall those four days the two of us spent together in Nanjing.

When we arrived in Shanghai, my father avoided attending his cousin's wedding party by taking me with him to Nanjing. It was only a short train journey. He called in at the High School where he had been offered a job as an English teacher. This was a school established by his alma mater, the Dongnan or Southeastern University, now the National Central University, the same one that he hoped I could get into. The university had followed the central government to Chongqing in 1937 when the Japanese forced Chiang Kai-shek to evacuate Nanjing. After eight years of refuge, it had just begun to settle back on its old campus on Chengxian Street 成贤街. When we visited it, we were told that the university was now much larger and there was the medical school campus in Dingjiaqiao 丁家桥 where the freshmen would spend their first year.

My father had me registered for the university's entrance examinations and wanted to make sure that I understood what was required. He knew that the examination was a challenge to me because I had gone to an English school. He knew I could not do well in the science paper because

I had missed many years of formal schooling, and Anderson School had offered too little on science subjects. Furthermore, I was not confident with technical terms in Chinese, having studied the subjects in English. In any case, he had me apply for the Department of Foreign Languages, where the English language would be key. He thought that, if I did well in that, all I needed was to pass the other papers. His worry was the paper in Chinese. The National Central University was renowned for its emphasis on Classical Chinese and, given the high standards required in this subject, he was not sure that I would do well enough.

Nanjing was busy with people adjusting to the new conditions after nearly eight years of Japanese rule. The organs of central government had returned from Chongqing. The economy was suffering from severe inflation and everyone was desperate to find ways to secure their livelihood. My father talked to me about the widespread regret among the people that the two major political parties could not agree to a coalition government. Everyone had hoped for peace, but the People's Liberation Army (PLA) had marched into Central Manchuria with the support of Soviet forces, and the national government was determined to eject them. My father explained why, in early 1946 and less than a year after the end of the war, this civil war was seen as unavoidable. Despite knowing that, he had been determined to come home because he was hopeful that the national government would win. Now the fighting in northern China was fierce. It was obvious that the PLA was popular in the rural countryside and much more formidable than expected.

My father had not been to Nanjing for over twenty years. The city had changed a great deal. He was tense about the mood people were in and seemed undecided what he should talk to me about the current state of the Nationalist government. Nevertheless, he had broken his silence about the politics of China.

After dealing with the chores he needed to do, my father took me to visit the Sun Yat-sen Mausoleum. This was built years after he left China and he had never seen it himself. He was also eager for me to connect with the revolution that had offered a new national vision for China during the years when he lived abroad. By telling me about Sun Yat-sen, who made Nanjing his provisional capital in Nanjing in the first months of 1912 and had asked to be buried there, my father wanted his foreign-born son to understand how he felt about missing the new regime's few good years after 1928. I had already heard a lot about the revolution of 1911. Standing at the foot of the mausoleum steps, I remembered how I used to boast to my friends in Ipoh that the date of the Wuchang uprising, 10 October, was one day after my birthday.

The side of the Zijin (Purple) Mountain leading to the mausoleum was a steep climb. My father showed me how to pay proper respect at Sun Yat-sen's tomb. The walk up and my sense of awe reminded me that I was born two years after the Guomindang government under Chiang Kai-shek was established and my name is spelt the way it is because my father had followed the official romanization adopted by the Ministry of Education of this new government. Otherwise Gungwu would have been Kengwu or Gengwu. My father began to tell me that Nanjing was not only the new national capital but was also to become the *modern* centre of an ancient Chinese civilization. And, standing in front of the tomb, he made me feel that Sun Yat-sen's dreams for a united China was at last being fulfilled. I knew from that moment that those dreams would always be relevant to my life.

The thought nudged me to think of studying with greater purpose. I must get to university as planned. But my options were limited and relied on my strength in English to gain a place. Of course, this was not so bad because it would allow me to pursue my love of literature, something my father had encouraged. My mother remained unimpressed. She thought that, with my foreign language skills, there must be better ways to serve the country.

The trip to the mausoleum led my father to talk about modern history, something new to me. Now, standing before the tomb and hearing my father tell the stories as he saw them, everything seemed to sink home. This was real and we were part of the unfolding story, with Nanjing once again the capital that Sun Yat-sen wanted for the new China. Nothing that day could have prepared me for what I was to experience a few months later. With my father's words still fresh in my mind, I would soon see the picture he painted turning colour, from bright to darkness. After being a student for a few months and wandering around Nanjing with my friends, I began to see a corrupt and demoralized government unravelling before my eyes.

The next day we walked the streets of Nanjing city and my father continued to talk about the 1911 revolution. In his view, that had given the Chinese people the opportunity to reassess their heritage and develop new ideas and institutions to catch up with the progressive West by opening their minds to new kinds of knowledge. It was not going to be easy, and the future was now connected with the civil war going on around us. I knew enough Chinese history to understand that winning the Mandate of Heaven required victory on the battlefield. The two sides were therefore fighting each other in the name of revolution for total control. That was the original meaning of the *geming* now used to translate revolution.

My father reminded me of the photographs of Sun Yat-sen in many buildings in Ipoh that were accompanied by his famous words, "the revolution is not yet successful, comrades must keep up the struggle" 革命尚未成功, 同志仍须努力. In Malaya, my father had not wanted me to be excited by that part of China's modern past. During the years he was preparing me to return to China, he distinguished between that *geming* and the military arm of the Malayan Communist Party's call for a war to liberate Malaya. The MCP took as its model the Chinese Communist Party (CCP) that was at war with the national government in Nanjing. Looking back, I realize how shallow my understanding was. Not many months after my father spoke about Sun Yat-sen, I began to doubt if the 1912 revolution ever succeeded and wondered whether the next one might have a better chance of success under the CCP. I began to ask if the Chinese people would have a better chance for peace and predictability if that party were given a try.

My father took me to see places that he remembered. Some were sites dating back to the time when Nanjing had been the capital of kingdoms like Wu of the Three Kingdoms period, the four Southern dynasties of the 5th and 6th centuries and briefly that of the Ming a thousand years afterwards. We passed places that more recently, in the 19th century, had been used by Hong Xiuquan 洪秀全 and his fellow Christians when Nanjing was the capital of the Taiping Heavenly Kingdom. He also pointed out places associated with the puppet regime of Wang Ching-wei under Japanese control. When he was telling me about that, he also told me that the local press was still comparing the fates of two of Wang

Ching-wei's chief lieutenants, both of whom had once been supporters of the Nationalist Party. Chen Gongbo 陈公博 was executed in 1946 while Zhou Fohai's 周佛海 sentence was to be commuted to life imprisonment. The country was wondering why the two received different treatments. Wang Ching-wei himself, however, died in 1944 before the war ended and escaped having to face the war tribunal. His wife Chen Bijun, who was from Penang in Malaya, was less fortunate and spent the rest of her life in prison.

He told me about the supporters of Wang Ching-wei in Perak and mentioned Chen Bijun's brother in Ipoh, and about the complex relationships among the local Chinese community leaders in Malaya before, during and after the war. In particular, he expressed fears about what the conflict between the Guomindang and the Communists would do to Chinese education. I did not fully grasp what he was saying about the underlying problems within the community. Years later, when he was visiting schools in remote parts of Perak during the Malayan emergency, I asked him what could be done to protect his educational ideals. He was his taciturn self again and simply said that he was doing his best, but did not share his thoughts with me as he had done in Nanjing. I was left to imagine the depth of his concerns as he struggled on for a few more years before taking early retirement.

We also visited his friend and fellow alumni, Mr Qiao Yifan, the principal of Zhongnan High School, who told us about the grim conditions in the city. Corruption in the government was endemic and the civil war was draining the state of its resources. There was not enough revenue to pay the civil service, least of all to help its officials keep up with the rising rate of inflation. Most people in Nanjing felt that they had gained little from the return of the Guomindang leaders from Chongqing. Among the grievances he mentioned was one that caught my attention because it was connected with something that had troubled me as a boy in Ipoh. He referred to the lack of attention given to the families of the victims of the rape of Nanjing in 1937. Mr Qiao told us that people in Nanjing were upset that more was not being done for the families involved. My father thought that this was because the government was distracted by the civil war and had decided that the issue could wait.

—◁◇◆◇▷—

At the time, most Chinese people had more on their minds than higher education. The most prominent stories for people in Nanjing were probably those concerning the progress of the ongoing civil war. The daily newspapers kept telling us that the government was determined to crush communist rebels and each bit of success was reported with words of encouragement. These were clearly posted from the Nationalist point of view, and my father alerted me to alternative views about the challenges facing the government.

He also cautioned me about strong measures against Nanjing university students a few months earlier, including police action on campuses like National Central University, and he told me that several student leaders were in jail. The main issues were economic, about hunger and the inflationary conditions, but students had also demonstrated against the government's dependence on American support in fighting the communists, including anger at an American soldier's rape of a female student in Beijing. By the summer of 1947, a ban against demonstrations in Nanjing had brought some peace to the streets, but there were still reports of union-led workers seeking higher wages to counter the high rate of inflation that troubled everyone's daily lives.

Talk about civil war was not new to me. Ever since my parents began to prepare me to return to China, the Chinese people seemed to have been in an unending state of war. My parents had grown up with civil war being fought close to their respective hometowns in Jiangsu province, and the resumption of civil war in 1946 was unsurprising to their generation. It was more a matter of regret that no other way had been found to resolve differences, and that a national government dedicated to post-war reconstruction proved to be impossible. My parents clearly shared that feeling, but did not talk to me about who they thought were responsible for starting the fighting again. When I arrived in Nanjing, I thought that the Nationalists had a clear advantage and would ultimately win, but I soon heard about corruption in high places and how the government paid its soldiers poorly and was unable to inspire them to fight against the People's Liberation Army. Even more disturbing was the picture of a deeply unhappy society plagued by rising prices that rendered the currency almost worthless.

I had experienced inflation during the last year of the Japanese occupation in Malaya, when rice had become very expensive and many people survived eating sweet potatoes or tapioca. Many people used raw greasy palm oil for cooking, and the price of fresh vegetables was rising daily. We were lucky to be living with a family whose workers were able to put edible meals on the table, but we were conscious that the Japanese were steadily printing more currency notes, and their value was falling.

I knew something about the subject from monitoring short-wave news broadcasts in English, which explained that Japanese money would not be accepted after the British returned. I also learnt about currency depreciation and its impact on daily life, lessons that proved useful in Nanjing. I could understand why my parents were able to survive in Nanjing on my father's low salary and still help his family in Taizhou. He had savings in Malayan dollars and was wisely changing his money a little at a time to keep up with the falling exchange rates. He taught me to do this too. After he returned to Malaya, he sent me a draft each month that was the equivalent of fifteen Hong Kong dollars. My uncle in Shanghai taught me to change only a dollar at a time, each time for a large bundle of the national *fabi* 法币 notes that lost value almost daily. For many, this was the index of the Nationalist government's loss of credibility. It was widely believed that the ruling elites and canny businessmen were converting their money into US dollars or gold bars while the rest of the population became steadily more desperate.

The situation continued to deteriorate. By the summer of 1948, one US dollar was worth some eleven million yuan, a meaningless amount that could buy very little. The Nanjing government finally replaced the *fabi* altogether with a new *jinyuanjuan* 金元卷, with an exchange rate of three million (*fabi*) yuan to one *jinyuanjuan*. I was in Shanghai that summer staying with my uncle, and from his office in the middle of the city we watched crowds lining up outside the bank across the road to change their money. After we changed some ourselves, we found that there was nothing we could buy with the new currency. All shops were ordered to remain open, but the shelves were bare. We were told the shop owners had moved all their goods out during the night. To our dismay, we could not even find a place to eat because the eating-shops and stalls had nothing to offer.

The mayor of Shanghai was Chiang Ching-kuo 蒋经国, the son of Chiang Kai-shek. He ordered everyone to change their US dollars and gold coins and gold bars for *jinyuanjuan*, and threatened to execute anyone caught with gold and dollars in their possession. Although I had become blasé about currency fluctuations after a year in Nanjing, I was nevertheless astonished by the confusion and fear that spread through the city. If I had any remaining hope that the Guomindang regime would survive, that summer removed it altogether. Like all my university friends, I became certain that the fall of the regime was inevitable.

Many years later I came across studies that revealed the full scale of the disastrous inflationary spiral, but from the moment I first visited Nanjing, it was clear that inflation was a serious problem. My father admitted to me, just before he returned to Malaya in March 1948, that he was deeply worried. Unless the government could achieve a quick and decisive victory in the ongoing civil war, the country was on the brink of collapse. I remember being alarmed by the sharp difference between what he told me then and his optimistic tone the summer earlier, when we saw people who were, at least on the surface, still engaged in making Nanjing once again the great capital of a new China.

There was no escaping the fact that China was again in a winner-take-all bitter struggle to establish who should be the new "emperor" of a unified country. Coming from outside China, I did not want to take sides, although I knew my mother's preference was for a Guomindang victory. My hope, and I think also my father's, was that all could be decided sooner rather than later, allowing the country to get on with badly needed reconstruction after years of fighting and destruction. I had no idea which side would provide better governance, but as it became clear that the Nationalists were losing, I could understand why so many people around me were saying that the communists could not be worse.

Five Months with My Parents

I CANNOT RECALL what I expected when I left Malaya to go to Nanjing. My parents' long wait to return and the preparations for me to study there left me feeling certain that I would have a fruitful time. Uppermost in my mind was that my father's university was located there and that Nanjing as a capital dated back 1,800 years to the Wu state of the Three Kingdoms period. As a boy, I like many others felt sympathetic to the rival state of Shu 蜀, with its heroic trio of Liu Bei, Guan Yu and Zhang Fei 刘备,关羽,张飞, supported by the great strategist Zhuge Liang 诸葛亮. In Nanjing, though, I saw that I should give credit to the Wu state rulers, who recognized the potential of Nanjing's location. The city survived as a capital for at least three centuries during the period of North-South division, and from 1368 to 1912 was one of the two capitals of the Ming and Qing empires. And the Guomindang made it the national capital after they took power in 1928.

That did not mean that I knew what to look out for in the city. There were sites associated with famous poets, and places that recalled the exploits of good mandarins and brave warriors. There were horror stories about the Taiping Heavenly Kingdom, which slaughtered literati families when they made Nanjing their Heavenly capital, and accounts of their leaders killing one another even before the Qing armies began to execute every rebel leader they caught. Imperial examination candidates had stayed in the Confucian Temple district, purportedly preparing for their ordeals, but the district was well known for the numerous courtesans and entertainers, who looked after their extra-curricular needs. My fellow students took me to various places to help me soak up bits of imperial and literati culture, and I came to realize that being modern in China involved blending past and present.

The poetry associated with the city attracted me most. My father had encouraged me to read Tang poems, and they captured the past glories of former capital cities and the meetings and partings that were standard fare among literati in those times. Li Bo's poems had the added excitement of various stages of drunken abandon. But the poem most closely associated with Nanjing that captured my heart was one that was not part of the Tang collection. First pointed out to me by a friend, it was the lovely *ci*-poem by Li Yu 李煜, the last ruler of the Southern Tang dynasty with its capital at Nanjing, who surrendered to the Song in 975 and was later forced to commit suicide. It was his *Yumeiren* 虞美人. I have seen several translations in recent years, and particularly like that by Yang Xianyi 杨宪益 and his wife, Gladys, which reminds me of how I came to feel about the fall of Nanjing.

> There is no end to moonlit autumns or flowery springs,
> And I have known so very many things.
> From my turret the wind was in the east again last night.
> A lost land was too much to bear: I turned from the moonlight.
> The cavern rail and jadework wall are as they were before:
> Those rosy cheeks alone are there no more.
> Tell me, what is the uttermost extent of pain, you say?
> Mine is a river swollen in spring and welling east away.

Li Yu describes the sense of loss that overcame him when he was held captive in the Song capital at Kaifeng, some five hundred miles north of Nanjing, and recalled his former life there.

My father disapproved of the poem, reflecting his austere Confucian upbringing that frowned on writings expressing loss and hopelessness. He did not deny the beauty of the poem but rejected the sentiments in it as negative and not appropriate for young readers whose lives were still before them. Li Yu was also not a model for anyone with ambition, or a sense of duty towards society and a willingness to serve. He was thought to have been superstitious and self-indulgent and failed to behave like a responsible king. Thus he deserved to end badly. I noted my father's objections but continued to admire the many poems Li Yu wrote in the same vein. His poetry also made Nanjing, where Li Yu spent his happier years, more romantic and appealing.

I remember asking about the historical remains of the Southern Tang Kingdom (937–75) during the Five Dynasties period but was told that parts of the city walls might have become the walls rebuilt by the founder of the Ming Dynasty, Zhu Yuanzhang (1368–98), when he made Nanjing his capital, but no one knew exactly which parts they were. The palaces had been somewhere in the middle of the modern city but no remains survived. In the 1990s, archaeologists began to find Southern Tang artefacts in the Xinjiekou 新街口 district, more or less where people thought the palaces had been, but I have not had an opportunity to visit the exhibition that was subsequently mounted.

When I was studying in Nanjing, however, no one had the time to think of the ancient capitals, or much interest in them. Simply staying alive was a grim business, and it was enough that there were relics at the Ming tombs on the slopes of the Purple-gold Mountains, located in a beautiful valley near the Sun Yat-sen Mausoleum east of the city, where people could escape briefly from the dismal present.

My parents were living in quarters provided by my father's school. This was not far from the Dingjiaqiao dormitories where our freshmen class was staying. Their home was part of a row of houses with straw roofs, and walls made of wooden planks in the lower half and straw in the upper half. It was not as well built as our student dormitories, which had formerly been warehouses. We at least had tin roofs and wooden walls from top to bottom. Throughout the winter, I visited my parents every Sunday. The wind came in freely through the straw, and like our dormitory, their house had no heating. My parents were all wrapped up by late October but they were never warm enough. My father was teaching English, already an important subject at his school. He had a heavy teaching load, with lots of papers to correct. I helped with the corrections when I could, but it soon became clear that marking the longer essays produced by students in his upper classes was weighing him down.

My mother felt anxious but my father never complained. Instead, he would ask about my work and I would tell him how I was doing. He was always worried about my Chinese language and literature course, especially when he found out that my lecturer was an expert in ancient classical philology and particularly interested in the Book of Poetry. He brushed aside my assurances that I could cope and tried to alert me to things I should look out for. I would then amuse him with stories about some of my other courses, my teachers and my fellow students, especially the friends I made in my dormitory who ranged from aspiring engineers to students of fine arts and music. One of those studying economics was from our Taizhou hometown and aroused my father's curiosity. He was Mao Jiaqi 茅家琦 who later turned away from economics to become a historian of 19th- and 20th-century China. When we met again in the late 1980s, we found that we had many interests in common and became good friends.

My first year in Nanjing passed quickly because I was learning so much every day, probably more from outside our classrooms than inside. After we started school in October 1947, I had to cope with the stealthy arrival of my first winter. We were supplied with a warm winter long gown but I soon needed extra layers of underwear. There was no heating anywhere so I wore the same clothes all day and kept most of them on even under my bedclothes. Toilet conditions were primitive and there were no facilities to encourage personal hygiene. Everyone made do with the row of pipes and faucets in the large washroom that divided our building into two halves. We had high wooden walls and tin roofs, but cold air came in even through a large gap between the walls and the roof, even without the help of the winds that swept through. One morning, I found my wet face towel frozen like a sheet of ice and that prepared me to face the coming of winter.

My parents' quarters were within walking distance. At my mother's insistence, I brought my clothes for her to wash. Their place had even less protection from the winter winds, and like me they had to wear the same clothes all day, and had great difficulty keeping warm at night. I could see that life was very trying for them. My mother cooked and washed and tried to look content whenever I visited, but my father often looked worn and stressed. He was only in his mid-forties but had never been strong. Although he had grown up in China, he had lived in sturdy houses with an extended family most of the time. He told me that the dormitory he had in Nanjing when he was a student was in a brick building. Since 1926, he had lived in Malacca, Singapore, Surabaya and Ipoh, and had not faced cold weather for more than twenty years. This was his first winter after a long break, and now he had to deal with it as an older man.

My mother was always worried about what I was eating, but she had much more serious problems when my father fell sick. It started with a cold but he tried to keep up with his teaching and it became worse. I could see that the number of papers he had to mark was overwhelming. I helped him correct and grade the papers whenever I went home, but he did not fully recover and was at one point dangerously ill. My mother feared that he could not survive another winter and decided that they should return to Malaya. My father wrote to their Ipoh friend Mr Wu for help. He had been promoted and was chief inspector of Chinese schools in the federal capital in Kuala Lumpur. My father's successor in Perak had turned out not to be a success, and while political conditions had changed significantly since our departure, Mr Wu was confident that my father would do a better job. My father had in effect left the service, so Mr Wu had to arrange with the government to have him reinstated. My parents were grateful for his help.

In March 1948, the appointment was confirmed and my father returned as the inspector of Chinese schools for the state of Perak in the new Federation of Malaya. It was a painful moment for my parents. My father did not want to go back and he and my mother agonized over the move for many weeks. My parents felt, as did I, that I should remain in China to complete my studies, but I had very mixed feelings. I knew how much they had wanted to be in China, and how they had looked forward to the day when they could step on Chinese soil again. Was the move only temporary and could they still return one day? As I was staying on, I hoped to see them back again. My uncle from Shanghai took them to their ship. I had settled in, made new friends and was enjoying my studies. My father sent me fifteen HK dollars each month and that made me one of the richer students on campus.

After my parents left, the weather improved. I further explored the city and its environs with classmates who also wanted to know Nanjing better. Most of the students were strangers to the city. By the time my parents left, I had gone with my new friends to explore the city. We had started in the autumn of 1947 with the well-preserved Ming city walls and the beautiful Xuanwu Lake 玄武湖, both very close to our dormitories, and we went during weekends in the spring and early summer. When we were more adventurous, we went south to the Drum Tower in the city centre and further south to the Qinhuai river district, the old examination site around the Confucian temple that had always been a tourist attraction. Most of the trips were uneventful, but I did experience one painful mishap. On one trip, I borrowed a camera from a fellow student but a very skillful pickpocket stole it from me on a crowded bus. My friend was very understanding and, coming from a middle-class family in Shanghai, generously insisted that I not try to pay him back for the loss.

A large group of us organized a day trip to the Sun Yat-sen Mausoleum. Although I had been there a few months earlier, I went along because I also wanted to see the nearby Ming tombs where the founder of the Ming dynasty, Zhu Yuanzhang, was buried. Having grown up among southern Chinese in Malaya who still harboured pro-Ming and anti-Manchu sentiments, I felt the urge to show respect to the man who drove the Mongols away and tried to anchor a united Chinese imperial realm south of the Yangzi for the very first time. During that trip to the east of the city, my more knowledgeable friends pointed to several major public buildings, including where Chiang Kai-shek and his senior cabinet members had their offices. I was awed by the thought that the huge Republic of China was ruled from here, even as my faith in its leaders was rapidly slipping.

We were all conscious that our campus of former warehouses was unattractive and raw. A group of us visited the main Zhongda campus on Chengxian Street to see what was in store for us in our second year. On a separate occasion, we also visited the two missionary institutions, Nanking (Jinling 金陵) University and Ginling Women's Arts & Sciences College, both to the west of the Drum Tower, to admire their fine buildings. These visits gave us a clearer sense of our place in the Chinese higher education world. It was a good start for me for another reason. Early in 1948, a public speech competition in English for the universities was organized and each university sent two representatives and I found myself facing students from the other universities. I was one of two chosen to represent Zhongda and was very conscious that I was the only freshman to speak that evening. I cannot remember the topic I chose but I spent several days preparing the speech. On the night, we spoke before a full house in a large auditorium at Nanking University, the panel of judges included a couple of ambassadors. A senior student from Ginling Women's College won first prize and I came in second. The Indian ambassador, I believe he was K.P.S. Menon, commented on the speeches and added his hopes about future relations between China and India as two new countries in the post-war world. I remember being very impressed. My father was in the audience and highly pleased.

With my classmates, I made other interesting trips, including visits to some historic sites further away from the city. One of the most memorable was Yanziji 燕子矶 by the Yangzi river, where the Japanese massacred thousands of Chinese in 1937. It was a moving moment to have the killing field pointed out to us. Another was the strategic site of Yuhuatai 雨花台, west of the city, where many battles were fought in defence of Nanjing. The locals viewed the small hill as a memorial to heroic warriors. When we were there, we discovered that several of the Japanese officers who had taken part in the Nanjing killings during the war had been executed there.

I was learning something new every day, but I was increasingly aware that happy moments were becoming fewer as events unfolded. Even as we as privileged students enjoyed exploring the lively streets and unforgettable sights, we recognized the growing difficulties people faced making a living. I probably remained optimistic longer than most because I was unprepared for the changes taking place in a country I was supposed to see as my new home.

Settling Down to Study

IN THE SUMMER of 1947, I sat for the entrance examinations and sweated through three days in airless halls with hundreds of other candidates. The heat was bearable for someone brought up in the tropics but nevertheless uncomfortable. I did not know how many of us sat for the examinations, which were held simultaneously at several centres in the country, but I understood the competition was intense. That week was a mix of worry and excitement. I wrote the essay part of the Chinese language paper in classical Chinese, as required, but failed to grasp the moral of the quote from Confucius. I struggled with the science and mathematics paper and was not at all sure how many of my answers were correct. When the results came out and I was among the twenty-four selected for the Department of Foreign Languages, I was overjoyed. I suspect my English language paper had caught the eye of those looking for good candidates for the department and that pulled me through. Later I learned that the university had accepted only about four hundred freshmen that year.

The policy at the time was for national universities to accommodate all students in their dormitories and cover their basic expenses. Zhongda took few students that year because of the runaway inflation and financial crisis, and because the civil war had spread nationwide. Also, the university had just moved back from Chongqing and there was a severe shortage of dormitory space and overall facilities on the small campus. While the university included all the faculties and disciplines of a full-fledged university and was the largest in China, the total number of graduate and undergraduate students was around four thousand. Such a small number could do little to meet the needs of a country devastated by years of war, and this was the government's flagship university.

Our batch of fresh undergraduates was well treated. For the first year, we were all housed about two miles away from the main campus at Dingjiaqiao. There were three dormitories for the males, each housing about a hundred. The few female students had their own place further away and we only saw them in class or at social events, and, during the weekends, in outings to the city and environs. In my dormitory rows of double bunks were situated on each side of a large common washing and bathing facility. Eight students shared four bunks, and each of us had a desk in between the beds. Our group of eight included one engineering student, two from the Chinese department and one from philosophy. The others included two of my classmates in foreign languages. One was an ex-soldier from Sichuan who spoke with a strong Sichuan accent. The other was Hakka but, unlike those I had known in Malaya who came from either Guangdong or Fujian, claimed Jiangxi as his home province. I was delighted I could understand his Hakka and he was surprised that I could speak standard Meixian Hakka.

I was lucky in that there were a hundred young bodies in our dormitory and the place seemed to become warmer as the night wore on. We had plenty of company every evening because our dormitory attracted local food-sellers who offered us hot chestnuts and boiled peanuts. Each evening one enterprising supplier brought harsh gaoliang wine that he had warmed up for us. Although most of us were cash-poor, what was on offer was very cheap. The favourite snack for many of us was the gaoliang with peanuts, which warmed our insides perfectly just before we climbed into bed.

We had good lighting over our desks and there was little to do after dark except to read and prepare for the next day's classes. Our most common complaint was about the food. We all ate in a large dining room a few hundred yards away, eight to a table, with a regular set of four dishes and a soup. There was never enough food for eight hungry men, although we could fill ourselves with the rice available. This was a perennial problem and there had been clashes with the university authorities earlier. Students were not charged for food on campus and the student organization devoted its time to negotiating with the kitchen staff about getting full value for the money the government gave them.

As freshmen on a branch campus, we were aware that our seniors on the main campus were active in national issues of war and poverty, but we were a bit too far away to join them in their activities. We were very curious about what they were doing and looked forward to learning more about their causes when we moved to the main campus in our second year. Almost all our seniors had followed the university back from Chongqing and openly opposed the civil war. A few months earlier, during the summer of 1947 just before I arrived in Nanjing, several student leaders had been either expelled or arrested for leading huge demonstrations. That had dampened the urge to demonstrate on the streets but did not stop the protest meetings on the main campus. I was aware there were among us those who felt strongly, but they were prepared to abide their time and wait for the spring. In the meantime, they let off steam grumbling about the food.

I could never get enough to eat at mealtimes. My classmates had learnt to eat fast and quickly cleared the small portions of meat and vegetables on the table. What was really new to me were the tiny stones mixed in the rice that I had to learn to separate and spit out. I had to be very careful not to crack my teeth biting on them. My friends had mastered the art of sifting stones from rice in their mouths and spitting out the stones. I never learnt that art and thus eating for me was slowed down considerably. Therefore, I was relieved to discover that one could buy cheap and rich food supplements in the local market and sometimes brought to our doors by hawkers. This included large cans of butter and ice cream powder that had been supplied to China by the United Nations Relief and Rehabilitation Administration (UNRRA) as food relief for people displaced by war. UNRRA officials distributed them in the countryside but, as most Chinese could not consume milk products, enterprising townsmen bought them for a song and sold them in cities like Nanjing and Shanghai. City people and the foreign-born like me appreciated such food, and I ate these products when I was hungry at night. The butter was of excellent quality, better than any I had had in Malaya, and the ice cream powder was especially cheap because no one had refrigerators and few knew what to do with it. I discovered that, mixed with hot water, it made a sticky sweet drink that kept me warm at night. After several months of butter and ice cream powder, I put on a lot of weight.

Several other warehouses nearby were converted into classrooms. The students of the Faculty of Arts had classrooms close to the dormitories. There were more science and engineering students, and they had their classes with their laboratories in one part of this secondary campus. We shared four compulsory courses, Chinese language and literature, Chinese history, Ethics and a political orientation course named after Sun Yat-sen's *Three Principles of the People*. Most of the students of the Foreign Languages Department majored in English, but a few opted to study Japanese or Russian. We each had to take one additional language and mine was German. The routine for a six-day week was simple; physical exercise in the early morning followed by classes and then more classes after lunch. In the evening, we were left alone to study or make our own fun. On Sundays, before it got too cold in winter, we liked to walk to the Xuanwu Lake, just outside the city walls close by. Apart from making friends in our dormitory, that was the most enjoyable part of my first year.

English classes were easy for me but, as someone who had not studied in a high school in China, everything else was new. The Chinese language and Chinese history courses were demanding, and I found the Ethics course really surprising. Our professor was a Cantonese born in Peru who had studied in Europe and become an expert in German philosophy. He had a special love for Kantian ethics, which he spent most of the time explaining to us in Chinese. I confess I never understood him but one of our friends, who was majoring in philosophy, keenly followed the lectures and assured us that the professor knew what he was talking about. I was more interested in the professor's huaqiao origins in Latin America and told him that I was another huaqiao, but he was so focused on getting difficult European concepts across in basic Chinese that he did not show the slightest interest in the students he was teaching. At the end of each class, I could feel his relief that it was over. For myself, I was no wiser about ethics even after attending the whole course.

My philosophy friend who appreciated him was Yang Chao 杨超. He was steeped in the Chinese classics, well read in Buddhist sutras and key Daoist texts, and often compared what we were taught about Kant to similar ideas familiar to the Chinese. Yang Chao was enthusiastic and loveable. He was by far the most learned among us, and sharing space with him in our dormitory made me realize how ignorant and backward I was. He was to us all wondrously knowledgeable in several areas of philosophy. To our amazement, he spoke openly about having read Karl Marx and appeared to understand what the communists were trying to do.

I heard later that, after the CCP took over, Professor Hou Wailu 侯外庐, one of the Communist Party's leading philosophers, was so impressed by an article Yang Chao wrote that he recruited him from Shanghai to join the History Institute of the Academy of Social Sciences as one of his philosophy assistants. There Yang Chao helped Professor Hou with volume three of his *History of Chinese Thought*, the volume on the Six Dynasties period when Buddhist and Daoist ideas were in the ascendant. Unfortunately, when Hou Wailu and his team were attacked in 1968 during the Cultural Revolution, Yang Chao insisted on being honest and denied being a member of a "leftist" group planning to attack Premier Zhou Enlai, and refused to name anyone he knew who was. This exposed him to severe criticism from Red Guards, who then accused him of being anti-CCP. After that terrible encounter, he took his own life. Several of the surviving members of that team have now written to regret the loss of this exceptionally talented scholar. When I read that, I remembered how Yang Chao's face lit up whenever he came across a new idea or found fresh way of elucidating a point.

With the spring, some of the more active among us occasionally joined our seniors in their discussions during the weekend, and once we followed a large group of demonstrators onto the streets. The demonstration began in silence but as it neared one of the central government offices, the demonstrators began to shout slogans. We had each been given a sheet of the slogans to be used and some of us called out in unison. I cannot now remember the words but recall that some attacked the government for using American help against other patriotic Chinese. There were armed police along the way, some mounted on horses but, on that occasion, no action was taken. We were on the streets for a couple of hours and returned to the main campus.

There were also happier moments. In our group of foreign languages students, several were from Shanghai and loved popular music. They organized a choir and led us in singing popular classics such as The Blue Danube and Waves of the Danube by Johann Strauss. We met a couple of evenings a week and gradually moved on to more sophisticated songs by Schubert, and then well-known arias from the operas of Mozart, Verdi and Puccini. The arias were totally new to me and I had a lot to learn before I could appreciate them. Fortunately, the choir leaders were very patient. I was struck by how culturally Western some of the students from Shanghai were. Being with this group in the first year prepared me for my second year when we moved to the main campus, where I walked past the school of Western music in the middle of the campus every morning and evening. I often stopped to listen to the music students play their instruments or sing arias from Western opera, and envied their talent.

After the summer break, we returned for our second year and moved to the Chengxianjie campus closer to the centre of the city. We lived in large brick dormitories about half a kilometre away, and the facilities were much better than those at Dingjiaqiao. Eight of us still shared four bunk beds with two rows of four desks between the beds, but we had the room to ourselves. We had already met in class the year before or in the dormitory we had shared, but with our new closeness we got to know one another better. Every morning we walked along a narrow lane to the campus, passing two rows of bookshops that sold the latest books. Few of us could afford to buy books but we enjoyed browsing and, to my surprise, the shops allowed us to read the books. I was told that some students stood for hours to read the entire books. My friends and I were not so dedicated but even we were tempted to read a chapter or two when we had the time.

The four girls in our foreign languages class all chose English as their major language. One came from Chongqing, one from Shanghai, one from Nanjing, and one from the Northeast, where her home was being fought over in the ongoing civil war. They were all a little older than I was and treated me as their little brother. In our second year we were always together in our classes, and became better acquainted. They were primarily interested in language skills and all of them wrote and spoke English well. Their knowledge of grammar was superior to mine but they depended on the boys to keep up with the history of English literature. I wondered what happened to them after Nanjing fell and later learned that all four transferred to the Foreign Languages College in Beijing. One studied Russian and became an official in the Central Compilation and Translation Bureau; one joined Foreign Affairs while the other two did well in other government departments that required people with good English. When I met one of them again four decades later, I learnt to my surprise she had been active in communist party activities while she was with us in Nanjing.

I also began to appreciate why the university was highly regarded. The academic staff included some of the best-known scholars in China and they covered most of the disciplines found in the better universities in Europe and America. I was now attending classes in English literature. For poetry, we covered the classical poets from Milton to Pope in one course, and the Romantics in another. For prose, one course began with early novels from Defoe to Fielding, while the other was a special class on the 19th century that dealt with novelists like Jane Austen and the Bronte sisters, Dickens and Hardy.

Sadly, we did not get very far in our second-year studies. Less than two months after classes began, the civil war reached the northern banks of the Yangzi River. The university was ordered to shut down and we were all told to go home. I had little choice but to prepare to return to Malaya, but I had already made good friends of my roommates and become familiar with all parts of the campus. During our first month in my new dormitory, I had been elected chairman of the food committee. Our work was to see that the caterers did not cheat us. Two of us accompanied the kitchen staff to the rice warehouse to take delivery of dozens of bags of rice and check that the rice was not mixed with sand or small stones to increase its weight. We had to travel miles to the outskirts of Nanjing to take delivery and then keep an eye on the trucks all the way to the kitchen. At the end of the month, we were responsible for ensuring that the correct number of bags was returned to the warehouse. We had to engage three rickshaws to deliver all the rice-bags to the rice stores. Fortunately, our committee only had to serve for one month.

On two occasions I saw "action" with fellow students, who were increasingly disillusioned with the government. The first was when I followed a large crowd who marched out of the campus two by two to demonstrate against Chiang Kai-shek's dependence on American aid against the communists. This time, the demonstrators were louder and the slogans cruder and more emotional than during the earlier demonstration. In the end, the police were ordered to stop us and, when the crowd went on shouting, mounted forces arrived and forced us to disperse. I came away unhurt but heard that a few students had to be taken to hospital for attention.

Two weeks later, in the evening after dinner, a group of students held a vigil accompanied by speeches in the university's large auditorium. I cannot now remember what the central issue was, but I went with my friends to listen to our seniors talk about how bad the situation was. Halfway through the meeting, all the lights went off. In the dark, all of us headed for the exit. I left by the nearest side door but those who went out by the two main exits were met by young men with long sticks who beat them up as they came out. I saw that happen from a distance but did not encounter anyone hostile. Later, I was told that the men with sticks were thugs sent by a local youth group of the Guomindang to deter us from anti-government activities. At the time, rather than instilling fear they left me convinced that the regime was desperate. There was, however, little time for me to learn more. Soon afterwards, the university shut its doors, and those who could leave headed for home.

My Teachers

I HAD A MIXED bunch of teachers and was especially concerned about the professor teaching our compulsory course on Chinese language and literature. Her name was You Shou 游寿, and she was more a scholar of philology than a language and literature teacher. Her freshman course was totally unstructured. She taught what she loved and left it to us to make the most of what she chose to tell us. Fortunately for me, she loved classical literature and, despite most of what she said being well over my head to begin with, the affectionate way she presented selections from the Book of Poetry and the long fu-poems 赋 of the Han dynasty spurred me to make great efforts to follow her lectures. She began to notice me because I was so obviously trying. Unlike others in the class who were more familiar with the poems she liked, I was struggling to keep up. She became curious about my foreign background, perhaps because, as I subsequently learnt, she had taught in Xiamen and admired the founder of the university there, Tan Kah Kee, who made his fortune in British Malaya.

Professor You Shou was also fond of another student in my class, someone who could actually write classical poetry and was a fine calligrapher to boot. Qian Sezhi 钱瑮之 came from a distinguished literati family and had mastered his many skills since when he was very young. I think he was the only one among us who knew how good a scholar Professor You Shou was and admired her for her learning. She was small and rather plain and almost always looked dishevelled. She spoke with a strong Fuzhou accent and it took me a while to understand her lectures. Only gradually did I appreciate that what she told us did not come from the usual textbooks but were the fruits of original textual study. We were privileged to hear how she arrived at her judgments and why she thought they were better than the received commentaries. I was not conscious of this at the time but, on reflection, her example was my first taste of what it meant to be a devoted scholar.

The course was supposed to be an introduction to Chinese literature from the ancients to the Ming and Qing dynasties but she concentrated on the ancient origins of the language and on the development of Chinese poetry. I was disappointed that she gave me no opportunity to show that I had read classic novels such as *Sanguo yanyi* and *Shuihuzhuan*, but she did not get much beyond the Tang poets. As a result, my knowledge of Chinese literature of the past thousand years remained slim and vague for years afterwards. Fortunately for me, she did get to some of the great *ci*-poems of the Song, and they reminded me of what my father had said about his maternal grandfather, Chen Tingzhuo. However, my father was not himself keen on the genre and I did not know at the time why his grandfather was highly regarded. By chance, towards the end of the course, when Professor You Shou was explaining how *ci*-poems became so good during the Song, I mentioned that my father thought Chen Tingzhuo's *Baiyuzhai cihua* 白雨斋词话 had made contributions on the subject. She turned out to know the work well and this made me feel that I was no longer just a huaqiao and beyond the pale. It was my first experience of vicarious fame and I basked in it during my last weeks in her class. By that time, my father had returned to Malaya. When I wrote to him about You Shou, he felt assured that I could manage and encouraged me to learn more from her.

I never saw her again and heard nothing about her until 1993. One of her students visited Hong Kong when I was at Hong Kong University and brought greetings from her, and a gestetnered copy of some of her poetry. It turned out that she had spent decades teaching in a university in China's northernmost province of Heilongjiang. She had continued her study of the language of the oracle-bones, but she also became an expert on the history and literature of the northeastern tribes that were perpetually a thorn in the side of China's rulers. There was no mention of what she went through during the Cultural Revolution years but, after 1980, she had become a highly respected scholar again.

I was delighted to hear from her and sent her one of my books and even hoped that I might get to see her again. But a few months later, in 1994, I heard she had died, aged 88. Only then did I discover how she had come to be teaching a freshman literature course in 1947 at National Central University. I learned that she was a brilliant student of classical philology and had been appointed as a research fellow at the new 中央研究院 (Academia Sinica). She then had a misunderstanding with the director of the Institute of Philology and History, Fu Sinian 傅斯年. She had a stubborn streak and did not admit any wrongdoing and was ultimately asked to leave. She took a teaching position in one of the smaller universities in Sichuan before joining National Central University and moving to Nanjing in 1947.

Fu Sinian was one of the leading historians of his generation. He followed Chiang Kai-shek's government to Taiwan and became the president of National Taiwan University. While in Hong Kong, I had become associated with the Academia Sinica and learnt more about the senior scholars there and their achievements in classical philology. I could not help wondering whether, had You Shou not fallen out with Fu Sinian and remained with the institute, she might have followed some of her colleagues to Taiwan and become like them widely recognized for her scholarship. However, for me, she was the teacher who opened my eyes to the power of ancient words in literary development and, indirectly, also prepared me to approach the history of the pre-Qin era without trepidation many years later when I was teaching at the University of Malaya in Singapore.

My first months at Zhongda had opened my eyes to the new China that was emerging. What I saw and read every day was different from the idealized picture my parents had given me. It made me realize something obvious: that much can change in a short period of time and look terribly different even if the perspective is only slightly altered. My parents remembered fondly their youth in China before 1930 and hoped that China's recovery after the Sino-Japanese war would allow the past to be restored. They were keen that I identify with China and accept that I would live the rest of my life there. I had taken for granted that they knew best, and in going to Zhongda I not only attended my father's old school but also the best university in the country.

The university did make us feel that it was the best and that we were privileged to be there. We had been carefully selected and were seen as an investment in the nation's talent pool. We had free board and paid no fees. Each of us was also given two sets of changpao (a long gown), one for summer and one for winter. Conditions were not ideal after the long and brutal war, but the university did its best to enable us to settle down and study. It had attracted excellent scholars to teach there and they assured us that the university was proud of the graduates it produced. Our teachers regretted the civil war and admitted that the inflation-weakened economy was hurting everyone's livelihood and was the source of political instability. People in Nanjing were surprisingly calm and quietly adapted to adverse conditions, but all was obviously not well when our teachers needed additional jobs to make ends meet. While they saw us briefly after class, none made themselves available for long.

I remember being greeted on arrival by the head of instruction (xundaozhang 训导长) in charge of looking after students. Not being a product of a Chinese school, I was not familiar with such an officer but did know that the Chinese schools that my father inspected in the state of Perak were expected to have at least one teacher responsible for students' morals and social habits. Our head at Zhongda, Sha Xuejun 沙学浚, was a highly regarded German-trained professor who had published several key texts on China's geography. He was very keen on tidiness and commitment and offered injunctions about good behaviour. He alerted us to take seriously the compulsory course for all freshmen, the course on the book, *Three Principles of the People*, based on the series of lectures given by the Father of the Nation, Sun Yat-sen, shortly before he died in 1925.

I learnt later that Sha Xuejun was from our hometown of Taizhou and several years my father's junior. He had studied at Jinling (Nanjing) University and won a scholarship to Germany where he obtained his doctorate from the University of Berlin. In 1949, he followed the Nationalist government to Taiwan where he remained in academia, and later also taught in Hong Kong and Singapore. When he was teaching at the Nanyang University in Singapore in 1964, my father tried to arrange for us to meet. I was then in Kuala Lumpur and did not manage to see him, but I remembered him as a keen scholar who took pains to advise us on how to make full use of our time on campus.

What struck me most during my first weeks was that all our seniors seemed to have come from Sichuan or at least spoke Chinese with a Sichuan accent, while most of the freshmen came from the lower Yangzi valley. A large number of my classmates were Wu dialect speakers from Jiangsu and Zhejiang. For a national university, this was an unrepresentative group. It was explained to me later that post-war conditions did not allow students in many of the more distant provinces to consider taking entrance examinations in a university in Nanjing. The bulk of those who did take the exams came from the lower Yangzi. The intake was small because had the university admitted more from that region, it would have appeared provincial.

For someone who had lived all my life abroad, it was strange to be among people who spoke varieties of Chinese that were so different from my parents' speech as well as the Hakka, Cantonese and Hokkien dialects and accents that I heard in Ipoh. I should add that there was even greater variety among our teachers and I strained to understand a couple of them. On the whole, I managed to attune myself to different speech patterns, and the experience proved to be a splendid introduction to China. Most of all, the dominance of Sichuan "mandarin" speech on a campus in Nanjing reminded us of the ten years' travails of the university after it had been forced to leave the city in 1937. It was humbling to know how much our teachers and seniors had been through and that made me more determined to learn from them. The majority of my freshman class were conscious that they had grown up under the puppet Wang Ching-wei regime that had served the Japanese. They were eager to forget that unhappy period and move on, and no one wanted to talk about their experiences during the war. Thus I encountered my first experience of being with people who saw collective amnesia as something forward-looking and positive. This was quite different from the people I knew in Ipoh where those who wanted to forget the war were chided for not reporting every wartime wrongdoing.

I had looked forward to studying with my professors in the Foreign Languages and Literature Department. They included specialists on Shakespeare, on European classical learning and Sinology, on the Romantics, on fiction, on linguistics and translation. I did not get a chance to know most of them except by reputation because few of them taught freshmen. In my second year, I had just started classes with the experts on fiction and translation, and on the Romantics, when the university was disbanded. The Shakespeare specialist, Lou Guanglai 楼光来, who was the dean of the College of Humanities, did begin to teach us but only from Lytton Strachey's *Eminent Victorians*. We were not with him long enough to know why he considered that book important. I appreciated Strachey's style and historical judgments, in part because the essays provided a corrective to the British Empire history taught in my high school in Ipoh.

Fan Cunzhong 范存忠, an expert on European classics and orientalism, was head of our department. I never saw him but heard that he was a brilliant teacher. Years later, in 1973, I visited Nanjing and met him for the first time. He was then vice-president of Nanjing University. I told him of my freshman year under a different regime and he said he remembered my father as a fellow student of English literature. Fan Cunzhong had won a scholarship to the United States where he studied with Irving Babbitt, and was considered the most distinguished scholar of English literature in the PRC. My father had died the year before our meeting. I know he would have been delighted to learn that I had met Fan Cunzhong, and would have wanted to re-connect with his old Department of Foreign Languages.

The one teacher of English literature in my first year we all liked was Liu Shimu 刘世沐, whose speciality was the Romantic poets. We were young and the best-known poems were familiar to us. He was obviously enthusiastic and conscious that the Romantics were the poets to get our full attention. He told us stories about Wordsworth and Coleridge that were new to us, but spent most time on the life of Keats and on the classical references in his poems. This allowed him to introduce us to the ancient Greeks and to make us compare the use of classical images in some of the best Chinese poems of the Tang and Song dynasties. Without knowing it, he was indirectly connecting me to the lectures of my teacher You Shou, who started the other way round, teaching us the classics that clearly inspired later Chinese poets. Even at the time, I thought this was the most important thing I learnt in my freshman year. Looking back, I believe that what the two teachers pointed to in different ways influenced my later studies more than I realized, not in the way they intended, which was to heighten my appreciation of literature, but in the way I learnt my history.

I have been asked why I chose to be an historian and I have to admit that I did not make that choice until rather late in my university studies in Singapore. I disliked the subject in school, in part because it was all about the British Empire but even more because the teacher read from the textbook and was obviously uninspired. The General History of China course that all freshmen in the Arts Faculty had to take at Zhongda was another disappointment. Our professor, Miao Fenglin 缪凤林, was head of the History Department. He was the only senior professor to teach us freshmen and we all appreciated that. He was very well known for his widely-used university textbook, *Outline of Chinese History* (中国通史要略), which dealt with Chinese history from ancient times to the present. It was one of only two textbooks I bought that first year.

My classmates found him to be very conservative and some objected to the way he dismissed the modern revisionist historians of the day. The latter group included Hu Shi's students like Gu Jiegang 顾颉刚 and his friends, who produced the very influential set of Debates on Ancient History (古史辩). Miao Fenglin regarded them as too Anglo-American. He was even more contemptuous of those like Guo Moruo 郭沫若 and Lu Zhenyu 吕振羽 who were influenced by Japanese and Soviet Marxists. I had not read any of the works that Miao Fenglin criticized. It was at least a decade later before I began to learn about the works that the Zhongda historians criticized for trying to distort Chinese history. So I was quite bemused by the passion behind his critiques, and what he said did not help me accept what he was offering in his textbook.

I found his book difficult to read and was only superficially acquainted with the work of the "modernists" that he spent much time criticizing. My father knew him as his senior at university and advised me to persevere with his textbook. In fact, I was more attracted by the work of someone who had taught both Miao Fenglin and my father, Professor Liu Yizheng 柳诒征, the author of a three-volume Cultural History of China. My father had a copy and encouraged me to read it. Although no less easy for me to read, this work introduced me to a wide range of cultural developments from ancient China to the 19th century and provided fresh perspectives on Chinese civilization. It probably influenced my understanding of China's past more than I realized, but I have to admit that my formal Chinese history class did not lead me to greater interest in the subject.

However, although only indirectly, Miao Fenglin's lectures did help me to understand the course based on the study of Sun Yat-sen's *Three Principles of the People*, which provided something like a blueprint of Guomindang nationalism and was the sacred text of the ruling government in Nanjing. At the time, it was regarded as China's answer to both Western imperialism and Soviet communism. Miao Fenglin gave us a strong outline of China's dynastic and political history and the first set of lectures in Sun Yat-sen's book centred on moving beyond the dynastic state to the republican nation that the Chinese were trying to build.

I had encountered slogans of the Three Principles of Nationalism, people's rights (democracy) and people's livelihood when I was still in primary school in Ipoh, but understood little of their substance. In the plural society environment of colonial Malaya, the Chinese community was allowed to express their patriotism to support China against Japanese invasion, but they could not openly participate in political activities directed against the British. Accordingly, the nationalist credo in Three Principles was carefully played down although Sun Yat-sen's photograph was widely displayed and China's national flag often flown. On special occasions, the national anthem, which began by affirming the *Sanmin zhuyi*, was allowed to be sung. The young Chinese I knew in Ipoh were all familiar with the Three Principles, but, unlike in China, Sun's lectures were not taught. I don't know if the published volume was readily available in Malaya. I had never seen a copy before going to Zhongda and doubt if my parents had ever read it.

I was advised to buy my own copy of *Sanmin zhuyi* when classes began, and it was the second textbook I bought. All the other books I purchased were for my enjoyment. But, unlike the *Outline of Chinese History* that I struggled to read and never finished, I read all the chapters of the *Sanmin zhuyi* that our teacher recommended. I cannot remember what I found so interesting about the book, but it probably had to do with Sun Yat-sen's harsh words about what imperialism did to China. I had no political hostility towards the British Empire and merely found my school textbook versions of British exploits around the globe irrelevant. However, I knew what Western imperial rivalries had done to peoples and polities in Asia and Africa during the period that Sun Yat-sen focused on, the late 19th century, and the sharply different nationalist Chinese perspective on British activities captured my attention. I could see why the Nationalist Party was banned in Malaya and why the Three Principles could not be taught in Chinese schools there.

Many of my classmates at Zhongda refused to read the book. They were critical of the Guomindang regime and considered the book mere propaganda. The lecturer's approach certainly seemed like an effort to indoctrinate us with the official faith, although he did not appear particularly committed to his task. The examination at the end of the year was perfunctory and everyone passed. However, I was fascinated by what I read because, unlike the others who had grown up with bitter political debates and were inclined to take sides or become either cynical or indifferent, I was relatively innocent where China's politics was concerned. As a result, Sun Yat-sen's ideas sounded new and thus had a strong impact on me, probably more than anything else I learnt in that first year. It was not a subject that I liked. The numerous literary texts in Chinese and English I was introduced to were much more enjoyable. Later, I realized that absence of any political rhetoric in our education in Malaya made the arguments in the book seem powerful. I read Sun Yat-sen quite uncritically, and it was many years before I was equipped to understand why he appealed to some and not at all to others.

One reason that Sun Yat-sen appealed to Chinese in Malaya was that he had an overseas Chinese background. He had studied in English-language schools in Hawaii and Hong Kong and had been active in Singapore and Penang. I recall being told that the British asked him to leave Penang because of his speeches calling for revolution. All the same, I had never met anybody who had read the *Sanmin zhuyi* or talked about its contents, and came fresh to the first set of six lectures on nationalism as the foundation for the recovery of Chinese pride in themselves.

What I read did not make me a nationalist, but it did give me a better understanding of the course of modern Chinese history. Sun Yat-sen went on in the next set of six lectures to describe the principle of "people's rights" or democracy. I found it difficult to follow his arguments about the history of democracy in Europe and the United States and his explanation of what freedom and equality really meant, but two points stuck in my mind. One was that the Chinese should not imitate the West where these ideas were concerned because such ideas had different meanings in China. The other was that the Chinese did not lack freedom. On the contrary, they had too much of it and therefore could not unite to defend themselves when people who were better organized and disciplined attacked China. Obviously, such an understanding was simplistic and superficial, and I was not inspired to go beyond the required reading.

The third set of four lectures, on the principle of "People's Livelihood", was incomplete because Sun Yat-sen did not live to finish the lectures. I was intrigued by the way he differentiated this principle from socialism and Marxism and, in particular, why he thought that none of the prevailing ideologies was suitable for solving the problems associated with China's agrarian economy. He was clearly sensitive to issues of land use and ownership and the plight of the Chinese peasantry. Our lecturer dwelt long on this part of the book as if to emphasize that Sun Yat-sen really wanted to find solutions for the poor and not exploit them in fighting the civil wars that would ultimately destroy China. On this particular point, my classmates were quick to point out that both sides in the conflict were doing the same and hungry peasants were the main victims. Thus, every now and then, I was made aware that young students in the most privileged university in the national capital were not all sympathetic to the ruling government's cause.

One source of discontent, I recall, came from the two additional books recommended as course readings. Free copies of the two were made available and I took both to find out why they were relevant to the course. One, by Chen Lifu 陈立夫, was his *Theory of Life* (生之原理). The other, by Chiang Kai-shek, was *China's Destiny* (中国之命运). Chen Lifu was a former minister of education and one of Chiang Kai-shek's closest confidants. Both books were published during the war, when Chen Lifu was a minister and Chiang Kai-shek was, briefly in 1943–44, the president of Zhongda. Many students objected to the books and the lecturer agreed that they would not be part of the examinations.

The *Theory of Life* was written to counter the materialist philosophy advocated by the communists and the scientism that prevailed among the scientific community in the universities. Although Chen Lifu was trained in the natural sciences and claimed to be influenced by the latest researches in biology and psychology in the West, notably the work of Henri Bergson, many students saw the book as anti-Marxist propaganda and refused to read it. I was intrigued by the idea of creative evolution but could not understand much of the argument in the books. The lecturer did not offer to explain how they were connected with the *Three Principles* beyond saying they were critical of what the CCP stood for. Chiang Kai-shek's book was a manifesto for national revival that helped explain the government's complicated relations with the Soviet Union and the United States, and why China had sought American assistance to fight the communists after the war.

When the *Sanmin zhuyi* course ended and I had, I know not how, passed the examinations, I realized that I had learnt a lot from reading Sun Yat-sen's own words and talking with my peers, who openly showed their scepticism. In a curious way, reading the book had moved me from the exclusively humanities circle I was in and introduced me, rather selectively, to elements of political philosophy and the social sciences. There was, of course, no rigour in the course, no lively debates or enlightening give and take that might have sharpened my mind to a different realm of knowledge. But the readings introduced me to elements of the social science disciplines that I later encountered.

The *Sanmin zhuyi* course made me conscious of several concepts that I had heard of when I was growing up in Ipoh but never thought much about. Neither the British nor the Japanese wanted us to know about China and almost everything I knew about my home country came from my parents and from the classics that my father so wanted me to learn. The words the course introduced that stayed in my mind and followed me back to Malaya were unexpected and even unwelcome, but they kept recurring and became real for me in many other contexts thereafter. The following concepts have been interpreted and questioned in many of my later writings, and I am struck that all of them first came to me through trying to understand Sun Yat-sen when I was in Nanjing:

Revolution	How did "revolution" compare to traditional "*geming*"?
Nationalism	What did it mean to be Chinese in a nation?
Rights	Why were other rights more important than individual rights?
Freedom	In what way were the Chinese already free?
Equality	What was equality as a slogan and in reality?
Republic	What could this be in the Chinese political framework?
Party	How could one political party be the Chinese state?
Capitalism	Why did capitalism appeal to so many Chinese people?
Socialism	Why was the idea of socialism attractive to other Chinese?
Marxism	How did Marxism differ from communism?

These words seemed to grow in importance the longer and further away I was from China. They refused to go away when I returned to Malaya, and I sometimes wonder if my ignorance about them played a part in turning me to the study of history when I became unsure about pursuing my literary interests. In 1949, Malaya was moving toward independence and fighting a guerrilla war inspired by communist successes in China. It was also a time when various nationalisms were being redefined and democratic socialism was thought by some to be preferable to the Marxist-Leninist internationalist variety. All the words above were widely understood, though not necessarily in the way Sun Yat-sen used them or the way they were officially defined by the Republic of China. Even while Sun Yat-sen's book, *The Three Principles*, was becoming irrelevant, the concerns of an Asia awakened by the efforts to end the age of empires and colonies remained rooted in these same words. The need to study and understand them became more urgent in the Malaya I returned to. Something I had not gone to China to learn was now part of daily conversations among the educated was almost everywhere. I was made to realize that the words were even more important to me after I left China than when I was an ignorant and innocent outsider studying in Nanjing. As it turned out, going to university there did not end with my staying on to serve my country. However, it did liberate me from my family and my early formal schooling, and from the inchoate hopes I had set out with from Ipoh in 1947. That was the first step towards enabling me to start my own life.

Learn from Friends

BEFORE MY FATHER left Nanjing, I told him about two of my dormitory mates who also loved Chinese literature. They were both studying in the Chinese Department. Qian Sezhi, whose calligraphy Professor You Shou openly praised, had an impeccable literati lineage. His family had produced several imperial examination graduates, and was highly respected in his county of Changzhou (Wujin 武进). He took a liking for me, partly I suspect because he saw this half-foreign Chinese as someone eager to learn. He taught me about the history of calligraphy and added helpful footnotes to supplement what You Shou taught us about the evolution of the forms and styles of classical poetry. Gentle, elegant, a bit gangly, I remember him most for being modest and kind.

He complimented my command of English. He could read English poems himself but with some difficulty and depended on translations. I was interested to learn how much of Shakespeare had been translated, and that he had read the eight translations by Liang Shiqiu 梁实秋 published in the 1930s. They included the one play that I had studied as a schoolboy in Malaya, *As You Like It*. I had found the language difficult and struggled to read other plays like *Hamlet*, *Othello*, *Macbeth* and *King Lear*. Qian Sezhi had read all of them in translation and the way he saw their relevance to him as a Chinese impressed me. While I took for granted that Shakespeare was universally respected, I had never thought about how his writings might appeal to Chinese who could not read them in the original. It gave me an insight into what universal meant that I never forgot. In fact, I began to realize that a good translation of Shakespeare might even be more illuminating than the original if the reader is not at home with Elizabethan English. And, for Qian Sezhi, Liang Shiqiu's translations were beautifully done.

I asked Qian Sezhi to teach me more about writing classical poetry, something my father for his own reasons did not do, and he encouraged me to try my hand. He corrected my early efforts and explained why some words were phonetically wrong and others did not have allusive power. But we did this for only a few weeks before the university closed in November 1948. When we parted, he left me a poem about our friendship that I kept for years, but I was a poor student awed by his poetic achievements, and did not try again thereafter.

My other Chinese literature roommate was temperamentally different. His name was Zhang Xiong 章熊, at sixteen the youngest in our batch of freshmen. He too had fine calligraphic skills and knew his classical poetry, but coming from Shanghai and more open to the work of a new generation of writers, he wanted to educate me about the poetry of Xu Zhimo 徐志摩 and Guo Moruo, the novels of Mao Dun 茅盾 and Lao She 老舍 and the polemics of the Left led by Lu Xun 鲁迅, for which I was most grateful. He opened my eyes to what excited the younger generation and introduced me to dimensions of the modern Chinese language that were unfamiliar to me. He was outgoing, always cheerful and remarkably optimistic about the country's future despite the near chaotic conditions around us.

For personal reasons, he preferred the company of the students of our English class and joined us in all our social activities. While he was familiar with English literature through the many translations available, and favoured the Romantics above all, his inclinations led him to be knowledgeable about 19th-century literature in Europe, especially the German romantics and French modernists. Through him, I learnt what young urban educated Chinese liked about European literature, the orchestral and chamber music they preferred, and the plays staged in Shanghai. He showed me that a great deal could be absorbed, localized and reinterpreted through translations. He admitted that he might not have gotten everything right, but the inspiration provided was unmistakable, and fresh thinking and creativity came out of it all. His enthusiasm for everything new was infectious and it made me conscious of the new dimensions of literary and cultural change that were taking place.

He taught me about a new literary world that my father did not care for. When I told him about Zhang Xiong, he admitted that he had been wrong not to let me read modern fiction and poetry when we were in Malaya, and encouraged me to follow my fellow student's advice about what to read. I think he had feared that, in colonial Malaya, I might have become too nationalistic or sympathetic with writers who tended to be leftist and anti-traditional.

After a gap of twenty-five years, I met Zhang Xiong again in 1973 when I visited the People's Republic during the Cultural Revolution, at the time of the campaign against Lin Biao and the "Duke of Zhou" (an indirect attack on Zhou Enlai). Zhang Xiong was the first of my classmates with whom I re-connected after leaving Nanjing, and that it happened at all was pure chance. I was in Beijing with a delegation of historians and sinologists from the Australian National University soon after Australia and China established diplomatic relations. Our Chinese host at Peking University knew that I had studied in Nanjing under the previous regime and that I had lost touch with fellow students from my time in China. He asked if I remembered any of them. I had been very cautious, afraid to link anyone in China with someone who lived outside. At his urging, I thought that it was safe in the Beida context to mention Zhang Xiong, a student of modern Chinese literature who I recalled had not been unsympathetic to the left-wing cause. The next day, I was told that Zhang Xiong had been located. He was the deputy principal of Beida's High School in charge of curriculum research and the senior teacher of Chinese language and literature. Would I like to meet him? Of course, I eagerly replied. That afternoon, I was taken to the meeting room of the Guest Reception building and there he was, older but entirely recognizable. And, what was more, as bubbly and cheerful as I remembered him.

He told me about his work at the Beida School, his special responsibility for Chinese language education there, and the textbooks he had helped to produce that were now used nationally. I was delighted to hear that he was doing well and asked about our classmates. He told me about those who were with me in Foreign Languages who had studied in Beijing after Nanjing fell. Two were now professors at the Foreign Languages

College, others in various government departments. I also asked him about Qian Sezhi, whom he knew well. He told me that Qian did not move to Beijing with the others. He had lost touch and only later heard that Qian returned to his hometown in Changzhou and went into teacher training in the local college. I assumed that Qian Sezhi's considerable literati skills were probably not appreciated after the communist victory and that, despite his immense talent, he had to be content with a local teaching position.

Zhang Xiong was obviously being cautious and I was similarly so in return. We limited our conversation to our recollections and some education issues, and we both knew that was for the best. It was enough that we were together and left alone for about an hour. Now that I knew where he was, I vowed to try and see him again. When I visited Beijing in 1980, after Deng Xiaoping's reforms had begun, I contacted him and through him met several other former classmates.

Years later, during one of our visits when Margaret was with me, we also met his wife and we went together for a day's outing in the Fragrant Hills outside Beijing, where we had a wonderful time. On that day, he reminded me of our meeting at Beida in 1973. He said he had been told that morning about my visit and was given permission to leave the fields outside the city where he had been working. He asked whether I had noticed that he was wearing dusty peasant clothing, and I admitted that I had simply taken that to be normal. He told me that our meeting had been observed and that, after he left me, he had to give a detailed report to security officials about our conversation. Fortunately, there was nothing amiss. For me, it was an unexpected pleasure, but the event remained on his record, ultimately innocent but nevertheless notable during those last years of the Maoist era. I was pleased to learn that he never lost his calligraphic skills. He wrote one of Su Dongpo's poems for me, in his fine *xiaokai* (regular script) style. I framed it, and have it close to me still.

After my first trip in 1973, my visits to the PRC have mostly been official, as part of delegations of academics or to attend conferences or make official calls on behalf of the University of Hong Kong or the East Asian Institute of the National University of Singapore. Whenever possible, I have looked for opportunities to meet with relatives and friends who lived in the cities I visited, and I did manage over the years to visit our Wang ancestral city of Zhengding and my father's hometown of Taizhou in Jiangsu province. None of the relatives I had known were there any longer, so it was never a question of visiting people I knew, more an indirect way of "seeking roots". Thus, I thought nothing about Zhang Xiong's suggestion that Qian Sezhi might be back in his hometown. It was not until 2010 that I had occasion to pass close to Changzhou, and upon making enquiries I discovered that, although retired, he was still there and was delighted to hear that I planned to visit the city.

We thus met again and had dinner together. He was eighty-three and my senior by three years, and he looked frail. He said that he not only did not go to Beijing with Zhang Xiong but also abandoned his university studies. I sensed that it had something to do with his family but he did not elaborate. Without a degree, he could only teach at a local Teachers' Training School, eventually moving up to the Normal College in Zhenjiang and finally retiring as deputy director of the local Normal College, which was eventually absorbed into the Changzhou Engineering University College. He had continued to write poetry and do research on a group of local scholars, poets and artists (many of them related to his respected grandfather Qian Mingshan 钱名山). Following the reforms that began in 1978, his work was recognized and he became a local cultural leader. When he died in 2013, his admirers published a volume of memorial essays that highlighted his contributions to traditional literary and aesthetic values. I felt sad that his lifework seems to have cast but a light shadow on the high modern walls of wealth and power that most Chinese now want to climb. But I am happy to know that his persistent efforts to remind his students of what has been lost is not totally unrewarded.

⟨⟩⟨⟩⟨⟩

When my father was still in Nanjing, he was very keen to know what I thought of my course in English language and literature. He didn't think I would find it difficult, but was curious about my fellow students. He was not surprised when I told him how well read some of my classmates were, and commended me for realizing that many of them had a better understanding of Western literature and culture than I did. When I told him that Qian Sezhi and Zhang Xiong of the Chinese Department had read the translations of Shakespeare and knew well the writings of several other European writers, he said that he expected Chinese students in the humanities to have read a great deal of literature in translation. Now I was meeting Chinese who read those writers in their original languages. For me, the eye-opener was to hear people converse in Chinese about the works of European and American authors and excitedly make critical comments about them. I also began to learn to discuss, in Chinese, translations of Western novels and poetry with friends who read them. It was striking how well they seemed to understand the history of that literature and tried to put them in context.

I had the good fortune to have as classmates, and in one case as a roommate, two friends who had an astonishing command of the English language, at least in reading and writing. Both were largely self-taught, one focusing on English as a language and the other using English and American literature to gain greater access to European literature. The three of us became good friends. Xia Zukui 夏祖奎 was twenty-three and Zhu Yan 祝彦 twenty-one, while I was only seventeen, but we had common literary interests and they decided to treat me as a younger brother who needed guidance. My father was amused. He welcomed their brotherly care for me and encouraged me to learn from them. I did not think of it at the time but later suspected he knew all along that Chinese students were intellectually more mature than colonials like me, whose Chinese was limited and who studied English for its usefulness rather as a key to European civilization. In contrast, the bright students from modern schools in China were likely to start with probing cultural questions.

Xia Zukui was an Anglophile who concentrated on the greats in English literature and savoured the evolution of the language from Chaucer to Dickens. He grew up in Shanghai during the war, when the city was under Japanese occupation for four years, and had lived under the puppet regime of Wang Ching-wei. His experiences left him aggressively non-political and he refused to comment on the civil war between the GMD and the CCP raging at the time. "A plague on both their houses" was, I think, on his mind. He wrote flawless English, his pronunciation was invariably correct and his knowledge of grammar and syntax was much better than mine. I was not surprised to learn later that he topped the English paper in our entrance examinations.

He declined to tell me how he became so good in a language that almost no one spoke and few people used. I could only assume that the concession areas of Shanghai were different, and that more people there used the language. What was to me remarkable was that he had excellent classical Chinese, having studied it from young. I soon realized that he had nothing to learn from any of the courses we had to take and was spending all his time reading on his own. He took every opportunity to show me the importance of tracing English words and phrases back to their origins in Latin and Greek, or French and German. I never knew how good he was in those other languages but was impressed by his familiarity with the grammar and structure of each and how they compared with English.

Among our teachers, he was interested in Lu Tianshi 呂天石, who had translated several novels by Thomas Hardy. I had read about Hardy in my father's literary magazines, but had not read any of his novels. Among modern writers, I had been drawn more to the work of Joseph Conrad and D.H. Lawrence, but I began reading *Tess of the D'Ubervilles* and *The Mayor of Casterbridge* in Chinese translation before I found the English originals. I became interested in the way Xia Zukui picked at the professor's translations, praising him here and there but also questioning his choice of words in Chinese. It was a new experience for me to hear a freshman critiquing his professor's work, and I was fascinated by how persuasive he was. He was a natural teacher. It was therefore not surprising when I later learned that he had become one of the best teachers of the language in the Beijing Foreign Languages College. When I met him again in 1980, he was the professor in charge of the training programme for simultaneous translators set up in Beijing by the United Nations. I visited him in his language laboratory and saw some of his students in training, and could see why many of them became translation professionals.

When we met thirty-two years after parting, he was almost unchanged, still smiling and cheerful and just a little plumper. He had all his hair with only a few greyish strands. He remained dismissively non-political and did not even concede that Deng Xiaoping's reforms had made China a happier place to live. He said nothing about how he survived the Cultural Revolution and refused to be drawn on the subject. He was doggedly professional, determined to serve to the best of his ability but refusing to identify with any of the official slogans and the party rhetoric employed to guide national progress. I saw him once more in the 1990s and then heard that he had retired to join his son, who was working in England. I believe that he could not have been happier than to be there, and it made me very sad to learn that, shortly after the move, a botched operation ended his life.

Our mutual friend Zhu Yan could not have been more different. He had taken the entrance examinations to National Central University after having just returned from a teaching job during the war years in a remote part of Yunnan. His family lived in Jiangyin, a county in Jiangsu not far from Nanjing, and I never worked out how he got to Yunnan. He was secretive about his life and background, and only told me that he learnt his English from an American who befriended him when he was a teacher in a Yunnan primary school. Apparently, his school was near the airbase in Kunming that the Flying Tigers had used to support the war against Japan. The American lent him some books and helped him borrow books from the airbase library. The most important influence on him, he said, was Walt Whitman's *Leaves of Grass*.

He had always been fond of literature but knew Western literature mainly through translated works. In Yunnan, he could find very few of them, so he began seriously to learn English so that he could read the originals. He made great progress after he began to read the American books. Whitman appealed to him most and he showed me his dog-eared paperback copy and proudly told me which poems he liked best. I recall it was "Song of the Open Road". But what intrigued me was how readily he turned to the literature produced in England. Unlike Xia Zukui, he preferred the modern poets, probably due to the effect of reading Whitman, and he introduced me to the poetry of T.S. Eliot and W.H. Auden. I was greatly humbled by his wealth of knowledge of contemporary literature. As a product of an English school with a father who encouraged me to read his literary magazines, I thought I knew something of the British literary world, but he showed me that my knowledge was conventional and patchy. Learning from him about Eliot and Auden was a small turning point for me. It opened a new understanding of contemporary writings, and English literature never looked the same after that.

Zhu Yan's commitment was extraordinary. This became clear to me when he took me to the British Council Library in Nanjing one day and told me about the arrival of the first copy in China of T.S. Eliot's *Four Quartets*. Although the book had been published some years earlier, I had never heard of it, but Zhu Yan learnt that a copy had arrived in the library and wanted to read it. When he discovered it could not be taken out because it was new and the library had just one copy, he sat down and started to copy the poems by hand. He could only do a few pages a day, so he went again and again for several days until he had all four quartets down in his exercise book. I had never seen anyone do this before, and haven't met anyone like him since.

There was yet another side to him—his love for Russian authors, especially Tolstoy and Dostoevsky. He did not read Russian but he was not content to read them in Chinese translation, and had turned to the English versions of *Anna Karenina* and *Crime and Punishment*. By the time I met him, he was in the midst of reading *The Brothers Karamazov* in English. It was through seeing the list of books he had read that I began to understand how young Chinese came to read the best of European writings. American and British missionary teachers taught the first generation to appreciate scientific and philosophical ideas. In the early 20th century, the second generation turned to translators like Yan Fu 严复 and Lin Shu 林纾, who concentrated on the social sciences and fiction. Next came those who read the latest western works translated into Chinese from the Japanese versions, followed by returned students from the United States and Europe who expanded the range of reading to include other European writings, including the Greek and Latin classics, mostly through works translated into English. Although the flow of such books was slowed by the Sino-Japanese war, the list of books available in translation was long. Of course, the numbers able to get access to them remained small, but even high school graduates could become familiar with Western works. Nevertheless, Zhu Yan's literary self-education was quite exceptional for someone who spent his youth in a small village in Yunnan.

In 1980, together with Xia Zukui and Zhang Xiong, I met Zhu Yan again. By then, he was a distinguished professor of German at the Beijing Foreign Languages College. He had switched to studying German after moving from Nanjing to Beijing in 1949 and graduated in 1951. He stayed on to teach the language in the East European Languages division and became head of the German Department. He specialized in teaching literature and led the team that produced the standard four-volume textbook in German studies used in Chinese universities. I sensed that I shouldn't ask him about his life during the Cultural Revolution, and he never mentioned the subject. He was quiet and soft-spoken, just as I remembered him when we parted thirty-two years earlier.

I also recalled our last meeting in late November of 1948, a few nights before I left Nanjing to return to Malaya. It was night when he said goodbye, and he surprised me by saying that he was returning to his hometown in Jiangyin to join his friends in crossing to the northern bank of the Yangzi. Clearly he trusted me, because what he planned was tantamount to joining the enemy forces beginning to mass in the north for a final push to take Nanjing. Zhang Xiong, who greatly admired him, later told me that Zhu Yan was an orphan, the son of a war hero who died fighting with communist guerrillas during the Sino-Japanese war. Although he remained non-political as a scholar of German literature, he was trusted as a patriot and highly respected by the education authorities.

Zhu Yan was my gentle mentor at Central University in Nanjing and, during those months we were together, he treated me like a younger brother. The night he left for his hometown, he gave me his copy of *Leaves of Grass*.

My Mother Back in Ipoh

" Ever since our country was victorious, our compatriots were ever joyous whenever we met and talked about plans to return home. Already several were preparing for their departure or about to leave, all with no plans to come back south. I cannot mention here all those who were also planning to go. We were awaiting the announcement of the results of your Cambridge School Examinations before making a decision, but we were already making the necessary preparations. Mrs Zhou and her family also planned to go after her children had each completed one stage of their education.

In March 1947, your results were published and fortunately they were not bad, so we decided that you should go home for your university education. Your father had always wanted not to stay long in the Nanyang but had not dared to resign because of the troubles in the country and the financial straits at home. In his heart, he often felt unhappy and thought this was a good time to return for good. He would first ask for leave and then later resign. Once this was decided, your fourth granduncle in Nanjing found him a teaching position. We had already been in touch with the shipping company to make reservations for the trip to Shanghai. Because the war was just over, there was still a shortage of shipping and we were not able to get tickets until June.

Our ship was very large and the sea was calm, so I did not suffer any seasickness. It was a smooth journey and took us only five days to reach Shanghai. My brother, my sister, our cousin and your father's brother met us at the docks. We had all been through so much since we last saw one another and there was so much to say that we did not know where to begin. We could only just laugh happily....

I stayed for more than ten days in Shanghai. Your grandaunt always loved your father and she extended that love to me. Your father and you returned from Nanjing to take me back to Taizhou to pay our respects to your grandfather. At his age, to have endured a life of so many anxious years of war, your grandfather was extraordinarily lively and that was wonderful. Although we had left home for eleven years, to see him again and to find everyone at home safe and well gave us great relief and pleasure. After a brief rest, we went to call on all the elders of the family. During the past ten years, several were no longer with us ... too many to mention in detail. Because there were still guerrilla activities in the countryside, we could not go to the family cemetery to sweep tombs and pay respect. This was something we really regretted. Two weeks later, for your grandfather's 74th birthday, we had a dinner party and invited our relatives to join us to celebrate. Everyone congratulated him and wished him a long and happy life, and he was obviously pleased.

After the birthday party, your father and you went to Nanjing so you could take the examinations for National Central University. There were many candidates taking the exams so it was not easy to be selected; out of some 20,000 applicants they only took 450. Luckily, you were no. 60 on the list and exempted from fees and living expenses. Although the amount involved was not great, it was meant to be encouraging. Your father had some business in Nanjing and you came home first. One day, your grandfather suddenly felt unwell with "flu". I did not dare to select a doctor so sent Shengwu (my older cousin) and you to your aunt's home to report what had happened and ask her which doctor to engage. Fortunately, the doctor's efforts were successful. After taking the medication he prescribed, your grandfather fully recovered and everyone was so relieved.

Guerrilla forces were active in the rural areas, but life in town was quiet and peaceful. This was not true for Dongtai. That county had been captured by the New Fourth Army and they dictated the taxes and grain contributions; people there could do nothing to resist them. My family did have some property that could have enabled the whole family to get by. But after eight years of war and with the New Fourth Army taking control, they had distributed their lands—the salt fields and their cotton fields—to the poor to show goodwill. Members of the family still felt unsafe, fearing punishment and no longer daring to remain there. They dispersed in all directions and lived among various relatives because they had lost their homes.

Thus I was unable to get together with my brother and sister to share our experiences during our years apart. We were in China for eight months but had very few chances to meet them and we spent very little time together. Till today, this makes me feel the greatest regret and sadness. At the time, despite knowing how badly off they were, there was little we could do to help. We knew we would need our funds to purchase what we needed to cope with the winter conditions to come, something that the teacher's salary your father received simply could not cover. It is hard to describe the predicament we were all in at the time.

Malaya Again

School reopened in the middle of September, so we said our goodbyes to your grandfather and left for Nanjing. Because the teachers' quarters were not ready, we first went to Yangzhou to the Zhang household to call on your aunt (mother's sister-in-law). The next day, your father took you to go ahead to Nanjing while I stayed on in Yangzhou for another three weeks. When our quarters were ready, you came to bring me there. The newly built house was plain, like a refugee camp, and it felt cold even before the winter had come. It had a thatched roof and mud floors. There were two comparatively large rooms, but the one at the back had only a small window that let in no light. The rooms were empty except for one bed, one table and one chair. The next day, we went to the shops to buy some simple necessities. Your father had started teaching so we could only shop in the afternoon and had to go out several times to get the bedclothes, clothes cupboard and kitchen utensils we needed. It all took us a lot of time and money.

We ate at the school canteen when we first arrived, but this was inconvenient and after a month we decided to do our own cooking. The canteen food left us feeling hungry, probably because it used too little oil. Although we only cooked one or two dishes for each meal, we found that the meals satisfied our hunger. After a couple of months, our life gradually settled down. You came home once every week and occasionally brought friends to take potluck at home. When we talked about the current conditions, it was hard not to be somewhat concerned.

The weather became steadily cooler. Your father was not strong and he feared the cold. Although we managed to keep going, we were afraid he could not continue to take it. He had long wanted to serve the country so he was prepared to endure everything and submit his resignation to the Malayan government. Good friends like Mr Wu and Mr Liu wrote to advise him against it and explained carefully why he should return to Malaya. Your father weighed their advice for quite a while and finally accepted his friends' kind advice to go south again. My sister heard about our change of mind and came to spend several days with us. It was a pity our living conditions were too poor and she could not stay long, so we lost the opportunity to spend more time together. Thereafter, we had to depend on writing letters.

Your father resigned to return to Malaya after teaching only one semester. He should have gone home to say farewell to your grandfather, but we needed to leave urgently. The weather was now cold and, although the journey would not have been very long, travel conditions were extremely bad, and to go back only to rush off immediately would have added to your grandfather's distress. We wrote to explain why we had to go suddenly and were unable to see him before we left, and to ask for forgiveness. We sent the things we had bought just a few months earlier to one of your aunts.

After everything was arranged, we left Nanjing at the end of February and caught the train to Shanghai to wait for our ship. Your uncle Bojiao and his wife gave us a dinner to send us off and he was very correct in expressing his feelings.

On the eve of our departure, a hundred emotions crisscrossed in our hearts. With the country in such a state, the family so poor, with an elderly father and a young son, the civil war tense and his employment prospects uncertain, your father recognized that he had no choice other than to leave. He told you that if the university moved, you should follow it wherever it went, but you can imagine the deep pain in his heart.

There were few passenger ships available and we could not travel directly to Singapore. We sailed to Hong Kong and changed ships there.

When we left, your aunts, your uncle and you sent us off at the docks. We were all so sad to part and took photographs to remember the occasion.

In Hong Kong we stayed in a medium-priced hotel to wait for our ship. It was very noisy, with mahjong played late into the night, and we found it hard to get any sleep. Because it was not certain when our ship will leave, we did not dare to travel out to see other places and lost the chance to see Guangzhou. There were other reasons for that: travel costs were expensive, so there was little to make us feel like touring, and we did not know that we would have to wait three weeks for the ship to depart. The ship was far from ideal. It was expensive and old. But because there were so few ships, we did not dare to miss it and just waited to board this one. The war had been over for two years and we did not expect such ships to be in such short supply causing so much inconvenience to travellers.

When the ship arrived in Singapore, the manager of the local Zhonghua Book Company, Mr Xu Caiming 徐采明, and his wife came to meet us and invited us for dinner. When Mr Xu heard that you had stayed behind to study, he became agitated and told us that we must immediately telegraph you to return south. His wife was sitting beside him and explained that he was very timid and would not allow any of his six children to go abroad to study, and thus limited their opportunities to advance their careers. We had left you behind at a dangerous time, and you only remained for another half a year!

That night, we caught the night express train and arrived in Kuala Lumpur the next morning. Mr and Mrs Wu came to meet us, and we stayed with them for nine days before taking the train to Ipoh, where we were met by several old friends. We had been apart for almost ten months and were very happy to see one another again. We stayed temporarily in Mrs Zhou's old home on Brewster Road that was being used by her nephew. By staying there, we helped with the rent and the household expenses, an example of mutual help, but the place was small and very noisy, and it was difficult to settle down. In addition, Mrs Zhou's nephew was experimenting with some chemicals that exuded a strong smell, so bad that we could hardly bear to breathe. When your father returned from work, there was no place for him to rest comfortably, so after dinner each day we walked to the Sanjiang Gonghui on Lau Ek

Ching Street to rest until about midnight before returning home. We did that for half a year.

You were in China studying well, and working particularly hard on your Chinese. Had you stayed there for a few more years, you would certainly have benefitted a great deal. In your letters home, you told us about all this and other matters at the university. Your fellow students did not trust the cooks to handle the food purchases and students were elected on a rotation basis to be responsible for managing food supplies. This assignment was not an easy one when the prices of all goods were changing rapidly—the prices at the beginning of the month were very different from prices at the end and it was difficult to predict the changes. You were only seventeen when you were elected to be manager, and you were responsible for the holiday period when students from out of town came visiting and needed to be fed and housed; there was suddenly an increase of some five hundred visitors. You seem to have managed and the students did not launch campaigns against you at the end of your term. This showed that, although young, you were willing to work hard and honestly had organizing skills. I was happy to learn about this and noted this down. Although we were living abroad, we worried about the civil war conditions at home and often could not sleep.

In Malaya not a day passed without news of guerrilla forces creating trouble, killing people and burning properties. The situation was particularly bad in Perak, and when your father went out on school inspections, he was often anxious for his safety. In addition, relations between the Chinese and Malay races were bad, and any small incident could have led to a conflagration. The Chinese government established a consulate in Ipoh and sent a Muslim diplomat, Mr Ibrahim Ma Tianying 马天英 to be the consul to try and help improve feelings between the Chinese and Malays. Mr Ma was warm and friendly, and charming and humorous in conversation. His wife was a gentle and dignified person who was the model of the good wife and wise mother, and greatly respected by everyone.

Mr Xu, an old friend, suggested that we find compatriots in the field of education who were willing to join a birthday society of twelve people who would meet once a month to lighten our lives and also add to our friendship. Each month, one member would arrange a birthday dinner to be held at the Sanjiang Gonghui. He would ask the chef to cook a meal that suited our tastes and help re-create fellow-provincial feelings, giving us pleasure during anxious times. Each of us would only pay $3, so it was inexpensive and beneficial. We also played a few rounds of mahjong and enjoyed one another's company, helping us all to forget our worries. This arrangement continued even after we moved from Ipoh to Kuala Lumpur, and only stopped in the 1970s, a total period of some twenty years.

In October 1948, the civil war made the situation in China very tense. When Xuzhou 徐州 fell, we knew that the situation was grim. Every time we read in the newspapers about the fate of refugees and the chaotic conditions, it caused us great distress. I wrote again and again asking you to return, but there were many refugees and it was not possible to get a ticket for you. At the end of November, we obtained a bunk ticket that enabled you to travel with Mr Woo's eldest son, Ti Hsien, back to Malaya.

About that time, Mrs Zhou and her family also came back to Ipoh so we also had to find somewhere else to live. Coincidentally, when I mentioned this to a friend, she told me that two vacant rooms were available to rent on the first floor of her place at Lau Ek Ching Street. We went there to follow up and all was quickly settled. The rent was $50. It was also very near the Sanjiang Gonghui and thus very convenient for us. Although there were flaws in the place, it was still much better than the place at Brewster Road.

After we moved, we tried to find a job for Mrs Zhou, but Peinan School did not have a vacancy, so we could not slot her in there. Your father recommended her to the principal of the Girls Middle School. The principal was known not to respond to private enquiries, but fortunately she agreed. A teacher's income was small, and it was hard to support a family on that. Fortunately, Mr Xu was teaching the Chinese classes at the English-medium St Michael's Institution, and both Mrs Zhou and her son, Shao Hai, were able to join him to teach Chinese there. Each was paid $60 and thus added $120 to their income, which was a great help.

The university in Singapore was not yet ready so you sought a position at your old school, Anderson School, and were asked to teach Standard

Five English. Your monthly salary was $150. You also suggested to the principal setting up Chinese classes, and you volunteered to teach classes for Standard Eight and Nine without more salary. In addition, during the afternoon you taught Chinese at St Michael's Institution, so your workload was quite heavy. In your two jobs, you earned a total of $210. Each month, you took $25 for your own use and put the rest in the bank to support your study at university. You also deposited a few dollars each month in a Post Office savings account. You saved several tens of dollars there but, unfortunately, lost your account book thus leaving the money for the Post Office. You taught till the end of July and then prepared to go to Singapore to take the necessary tests for university. Fortunately, you were successful, and in early October, you entered the university. **"**

Ipoh

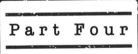

Part Four

Re-orient

IN OCTOBER 1948 I returned to Nanjing from Shanghai to start my second-year studies. My fellow students and I gathered in our dormitories and attended classes as usual. Everyone was discreet. No one talked about the battles being fought in the northern provinces, but we knew all was not well. For months, my parents' letters had spoken of their concern for the economy and the war, but they remained hopeful that the government forces could keep the rest of the country under control. This was not to be. Within a few weeks, in early November, Nationalist armies were defeated in Manchuria, and attacks on Beijing and, of even greater concern, the vital town of Xuzhou 徐州—about 100 miles north of Nanjing—had begun. This was when the university told all students to go home.

Those of us whose homes were far away stayed on. Another student from Malaya, Kuang Yuchang 邝誉昌 in the Mathematics Department, had joined the university when I did. I did not know him well but we now saw each other every day, along with a few dozen others who came from distant provinces in the west and the south. They had stayed in the hope that classes might resume after a while. Kuang Yuchang and I also learnt that two new students had arrived from Malaya. They were Malays who had received Chinese government scholarships to study at the university, Abdul Majid and Raja Nong Chik. They lived in a different dormitory and we only met them when our numbers dwindled. I learnt later that both followed the government to Taiwan and finished their studies there. When Majid returned, he worked for the Malayan government as an information officer, while Raja Nong Chik became a successful businessman in Kuala Lumpur. Kuang Yuchang remained because his father told him he should stay and finish his studies. Decades later, I saw him in Hong Kong and heard that he was unable to return home to Penang owing to the Malaysian government's restrictions on students who had studied in the PRC.

When my parents asked me to join them back in Malaya, I did not want to leave. Like Kuang Yuchang, I thought I should wait for the outcome of the war and stay on campus as long as the university continued to provide food and lodgings, but my parents feared that Nanjing would become a last ditch battleground and wrote again and again urging me to leave. They asked my uncle in Shanghai to confront me with the argument that, as their only child, I should not risk the turmoil that was likely to follow. He was very insistent, and bought a ticket for me to board a Butterfield and Swire ship sailing in the first week of December, so I reluctantly agreed. I have often wondered whether my resistance came from a sense that, once I left, it might be impossible for me to live in China again.

In Shanghai, I visited the Zhou family, who owned the house in Ipoh where my parents were staying. They had returned to China about the time we did in 1947, and I found that they too were preparing to return to Malaya. It turned out that I was travelling on the same boat as their

With my uncle just before boarding my ship from Shanghai to Singapore.

cousin, Wu Ti-hsien 吴迪先, who was visiting relatives in Shanghai and also pursuing his business interests. Going with him made it feel less like I was running away.

Our ship stopped at the ports of Jilong (Keelung) in Taiwan and at Xiamen before a longer stopover in Hong Kong. I thus had three chances to glimpse other parts of China before leaving. From Jilong, I made a day trip to Taipei and found the city orderly and calm. I only realized later that the province was under tight security control following brutal police actions early in 1947, and that preparations were being made for the island to serve as a refuge for the Nationalist government if the mainland was lost. At Xiamen, I remember the port as bustling with people trading with their compatriots in the Philippines and the Malay Archipelago. Everything was remarkably normal. In Hong Kong, though, there was some agitation. The local press reported that many businesses were relocating from Shanghai, including families who, for their safety, had a second home in Hong Kong. We stayed in one such place, which was owned by my father's Shanghai cousin, Xu Bojiao 徐伯郊, when our ship docked in Hong Kong for three nights. This enabled us to roam the city's lively streets, and we felt that the city might escape the civil war if the British remained.

⋯⟨◇⟩⋯

We travelled steerage on the ship and were accompanied by cargoes of salt fish and vegetables so that, when it was not raining, we spent our time on deck. I sat there in the fresh air thinking about friends and teachers I left behind. I recall being unmoved by the thought that the government would fall, leaving China under the Communist Party. Like many of my fellow students, I thought the regime had lost its capacity to rule, its leaders corrupted by power, and felt that China would be better off with a new set of rulers. It did not occur to me that the Nationalist Party might abandon the mainland and, with skill, luck and determination, re-invent itself in Taiwan. Even further from my mind was that its success would encourage the people there to dream of independence from China.

I was not troubled by the future of China as a country and expected China to be great again once it was unified. Instead, I wondered what I would do in Malaya, and began to worry about continuing my university studies. I recall moments of anxiety that I quelled by focusing on being reunited with my parents. My Shanghai uncle was right. I should be with my parents, who felt much sadder than I about China's prospects, and feared that the China they loved would be destroyed by all-out war.

As our ship approached Singapore, I thought more about Ipoh and my future there. I realized that I had not kept up with what was happening in the new Federation of Malaya. I knew that there was an "Emergency", in effect a war against the Malayan Communist Party. In Nanjing, the only news I received came from my parents' letters. They mentioned that my father occasionally visited schools in rural areas where the MCP was active, but assured me that he was safe. I knew my parents could not afford to send me to universities in the West, so I thought about the two colleges in Singapore, a well-known medical college, and Raffles College, which produced teachers for secondary schools. At least two of my teachers in my final year at Anderson School were graduates of the latter. I thought I might try to get into that college and pursue a teaching career.

It was with both joy and sadness that I saw my parents again in Ipoh. It was a week before the end of the year and we had been separated for nine months. How could we have dreamt that we would be back in Ipoh, the place we had so decisively left a year and a half ago? How had they adjusted to the idea that they might never live in China again?

They had been temporarily housed in two small rooms above a plastics workshop, but they moved into two rented rooms in a private residence shortly after I arrived. I was surprised they had not been allocated quarters, and was told there was an acute shortage in the town. Perak state was at the heart of the war being fought against the Malayan National Liberation Army. The post-war economy had not recovered and the government was hard pressed to build housing for their officers.

As I walked the familiar streets of New Town, I saw how much had changed since we left in the middle of 1947. The sense of crisis and tension in the air did not trouble me—I was never far from that in Nanjing. What forced me to think anew was the reality of being in the

midst of a fierce conflict about the future of a new nation that would be
built out of a cluster of Malay states with large immigrant communities.
My parents seemed resigned to this development and wanted nothing
more than to have me with them again to face the changing conditions
together. My return seemed to console them, and it was clear to me that
the decision to join them was the right one.

In a strange way, I soon felt at home, returning to a life close to
that I had grown up with. In fact, life in Ipoh was much better than
during the three and a half years of the Japanese occupation. I began
to understand why my parents were calm when they talked about their
hopes for me in the new Malaya. I looked for a job that would support
my future education. The principal of Anderson School was looking for
someone to teach English to its Special Malay classes and was happy to
hire an old boy of the school who had actually been to a university. These
classes were to enable the pupils who finished Malay primary schools
to enhance their English so that they could go on to secondary schools
that taught in English. I had not done any teaching in that language
before but recalled how my teachers had taught me and adapted that for
my pupils. I remember how we played word games and how quickly the
students learnt to speak and write the language. For myself, I discovered
that I enjoyed teaching and grew very fond of my two classes of Malay
boys, who were so keen to learn. I was asked to help with other classes
as well, and volunteered to teach Chinese to senior students who were
taking Chinese for their Cambridge Examinations.

In addition, I took a part-time job in the afternoon teaching
elementary Chinese in St Michael's Institution. This was the Catholic
school in Ipoh's Old Town, where most of its students were Chinese
whose parents asked the school to provide extra Chinese lessons.
There was such a shortage of teachers that, although unqualified, I
was employed because I had attended a Chinese university. Again, I
found it satisfying. My jobs teaching the two languages I knew provided
something of a bridge to help me adjust to life in what I now began to
see as my hometown.

I kept busy and earned enough to have some savings to help my further
studies. It was announced that the British government was sending a
commission of experts chaired by Sir Alexander Carr-Saunders to make

recommendations on higher education in the colonies. Some of my schoolmates who were already studying in the two colleges in Singapore came home to take part in the public debate about having their colleges merged to form a university. I followed the debate closely and was excited by the possibility of joining them. I found myself mentally preparing for a different kind of university from National Central. Most of my classmates were studying medicine, but I was not qualified to study that, nor was I interested.

The Carr-Saunders Commission, as expected, recommended the establishment of the University of Malaya. Raffles College would house the Faculties of Arts and Science. I applied for Arts and was admitted, together with my younger schoolmates who had done well in the school-leaving examinations. The fact that I had already been at university helped me secure a place. My parents were relieved and assured me that they would support me if I did not get a scholarship and my savings were not enough. I did eventually get a small scholarship that exempted me from all fees and helped pay for part of my hostel accommodation.

After July, when I was admitted to the new university, I tried to find out how this institution would compare with the one I knew in China. It was hinted that the university was tasked to prepare its students for nation building, and that the courses would take into account the needs of a future Malayan nation. I was dimly aware that the British were keen to ensure that graduates would learn how to run the colonial state according to British political ideals, but wondered what students were expected to study to enable that to happen in the complex plural society Malaya had become. For myself, I simply wanted to complete my studies and learn more about the modern world.

Both my father and I had given away our books to the university library in Nanjing when we left China, and I found that there was nothing to read at home. The libraries in the schools where I taught had mostly textbooks and the library club in town bought popular English fiction. I did find some books that I thought could help me choose what courses to take when I resumed my studies but I cannot now remember what I actually read.

A few years ago, quite by accident, I found a tattered notebook in which I had made notes of books I had read in Ipoh that year. The only date on it was January 1949, but the twenty pages of notes might have been made over the next few months, so I can safely say that they were my thoughts early that year. The notes include an unfinished poem I had written in English entitled "Ode to Yangtse" that showed a sentimental longing for China but was undated. Together with this were two random quotes in Chinese, one about the nature of true poetry and the other about how traditional Chinese literati judged what constituted good paintings. Neither was remarkable, but they reminded me how keen I still was at the time about ideas that touched on literature and aesthetics.

More pointedly, there were quotes from three books that I was reading, possibly in preparation for when I could get into a university again. There is no mention of where I obtained the books, but the quotes show how lost I was in trying to think about the kind of Western education I now expected to get. The books were J.A.C. Brown, *The Evolution of Society*; Karen Horney, *The Neurotic Personality of Our Time;* and Morris Ginsberg, *The Psychology of Society,* and they were my first excursions into knowledge areas I had not encountered before, sociology and psychology with doses of philosophy.

The following samples suggest what impressed me most in what I read:

- From Brown, "Society is simply a group of individuals arranged in a particular organization for their own benefit", "The State was founded by man for his own ends."
- From Horney, "The joy of losing oneself indiscriminately in a group is the most deadly enemy of freedom. People are afraid that freedom may mean standing alone, and to escape loneliness, they are prepared to accept even the most absurd and obsolete creeds." I also recorded several quotes about frustration and how aggression can be controlled, and added a note that seemed to sum up what I thought of her book: "she lists craving for power and excessive desire for affection as two of the most characteristic neurotic features of modern life. Both, she considers, are due to social insecurity."

- From Ginsberg, there were short quotes about repression, suppression, expression, sublimation, and neurosis and a longer one that says, "Although the State and other forms of community show a kind of unity, this unity is simply a relation between individuals based on community of purpose and ideals, and need not be referred to as a person or will. Men do indeed share in a common life and contribute to a collective achievement, yet nothing but confusion can result from hypostatizing this life and ascribing to it a reality over and above the reality of the lives which individuals live in relation with one another."

I was obviously interested in my own individuality and wonder if I had begun to sense the contradiction in what my parents had taught me. My father's focus on literature had encouraged me to think for myself, and attending an English school pushed me further in that direction. My mother, on the other hand, implanted in me a strong sense of duty to family but also an emerging national consciousness. Everything I experienced in China, from Sun Yat-sen to the Guomindang and the CCP, emphasized China's need for unity and collective effort if it were to prosper.

There are quotations from two other writers in the notebook, but it is not clear whether I had read their books or had merely found them quoted in Horney or Ginsberg. Several were about aggression, quoting William H. Sheldon's *Psychology and the Promethean Will*, and may have come from Horney's book. One of the quotes referred to the petty wars of the feudal ages being stopped by forbidding private armies and added, "The barons, no doubt, remained just as aggressive, but the power was removed. Similar action is necessary to take away the power of nations to wage international war." Did I think that was possible?

Other quotes came from Karl Mannheim but did not say which book they came from. I remember looking out for Mannheim's *Ideology and Utopia* when I was studying in Singapore and was very impressed by what I read. I suspect I had not read the book in Ipoh but found the quote in Ginsberg's book and made a special note of it. The central point Mannheim makes touched on an issue that continued to concern me for a long while. I include it here to underline something that was important to me during those transition months in Ipoh.

1. History shows a spread of neighbourly attitudes to larger and larger groups. Thus clan becomes tribe, tribe becomes nation and nation becomes empire.
2. At the same time, there has been an increasing isolation of the individual man from the community. On the one hand, this individualism has led to great progress in science and art, on the other hand, to neurosis and criminality, both signs of separation from the group.
3. At present nations are seeking a means whereby social isolation may be ended. Fascism and Communism are both attempted solutions of this problem, and show the desire of man to lose himself in the group. The question is whether a society can be built which will give the benefit of collectivism without loss of freedom.

The quotations here merely point to scattered thoughts about the world around me. Perhaps I contemplated studying subjects like psychology, sociology or political philosophy. That came to nothing because, as I later discovered, the Faculty of Arts in the University of Malaya did not offer any of them. It had only four departments, English Literature, History, Geography and Economics. For my BA degree, I had to choose three out of the four to study for three years. After that, if I qualified, I could do an honours year in one of them. I chose History, but that is another story.

I put my notebook aside and lost sight of it completely for sixty years. I have no idea how it survived my peregrinations after 1949. I can guess that these readings led nowhere and I had no reason to remember the books once I got to Singapore. But finding the notebook has helped me understand why, when I decided not to do my honours year in literature, I had considered doing economics instead. My study of economics had introduced me to other areas of the social sciences, and I was drawn to the writings of Marx, Freud and Weber, Karl Mannheim, Karl Jaspers, Pitrin Sorokin, Bertrand Russell and Harold Laski, and these led me back to John Stuart Mill and Herbert Spencer. But the honours courses were designed to train economists and that did not attract me. The quotes above suggest where my thoughts were leading, but they also explain why my contact with social science was so patchy and undirected. They make me realize that choosing to do history may have had something to do with my desire for something more open-ended. Although I eventually turned to ancient history and was drawn to Sinology and the classics, I found that I could not avoid coming back to some of the modern social and political issues that came to dominate the new nations of Southeast Asia.

Starting Over

MY NINE MONTHS in Ipoh passed quickly because so much was happening around me and in China. I was gradually distancing myself from the dramatic events in China and concentrating on getting to know the new Malaya that the British were hoping to establish with the Malay leaders. For the first half of 1949, trying to understand what the Emergency was doing to the local Chinese community that I belonged to was uppermost in my mind.

I was less innocent than I had been in 1945–46 when the Anti-Japanese Army came out of the jungle and supporters of the MCP joined trade unions to organize strikes against their employers. Now the MNLA was fighting a guerrilla war inspired by the successes of the People's Liberation Army in China. During my months in Nanjing, I had learnt about a guerrilla strategy that led to the growth of a formidable army when the CCP successfully persuaded many in the peasant and working classes to join them to fight against those who supported a corrupt and incompetent government. I had also experienced the demoralizing effects of runaway inflation and the financial fiasco of August 1948, when the new currency introduced was a devastating failure.

In addition, my exposure to the compulsory course on Sun Yat-sen's *Three Principles of the People*, however poorly I understood the book, had introduced me to the vocabulary of politics, something that my father and the education I received in school had carefully avoided. Taken together with what I saw around me in China, that course made me aware that abuses could negate idealistic calls for social progress. I had also become more sensitive to propaganda. The Three Principles course alerted me to the power of ideas behind words like nationalism, democracy and people's livelihood, but it also warned me of the extreme measures that political activists were prepared to take to capture power, and seek more and more of it.

One of the first things my parents told me was that as a result of the Emergency, political pressure was being applied to Chinese schools throughout Malaya. As inspector of Chinese schools, my father's responsibility was to assure the schools that they would receive government support if they kept strictly to their educational goals and provided quality teaching. My father was also very keen on providing teacher training to ensure that there would be enough teachers to meet the growing demand. He regularly visited the schools around the state to talk to principals and teachers as well as key members of school boards. Perak was where the MCP secretary-general, Chin Peng, had his headquarters and the party there had many supporters. With frequent reports of Chinese community leaders being killed, my mother feared for my father's life when he visited smaller primary schools in remote rural areas. He occasionally had to spend the night in a nearby town and my mother had sleepless nights whenever he made such trips. I offered to accompany him. My parents did not agree, but I insisted and did go with my father on two occasions.

The first was when we went south to three schools near Bidor and had to spend the night in Tapah. I remember visiting Chenderiang, a small town off the beaten track, where I was taken to see a beautiful waterfall near the local primary school. There were reports of communist activity and we had to go through several roadblocks manned by British soldiers and Malay policemen. My father insisted on traveling unarmed and unescorted because he was convinced it was safer for him that way. The trip was uneventful. My father called on all those responsible for the schools and we never felt unsafe.

Some months later, we made a second trip, this time to Lenggong and Grik in the north. My father planned to visit several schools, including one in the town of Kroh (now named Pengkalan Hulu) bordering Thailand and the state of Kedah. We were told when we got to Grik that the road beyond the town was not secure, so we did not go any further and spent the night in Grik. It was a long journey, and most of the way, apart from a few rubber estates, it was all jungle. I was surprised so many Chinese lived there. The community was mainly from Guangxi province in China, and had fought the Japanese during the occupation, not with the communists but as patriots in support of the Guomindang government. By 1949, the MNLA had moved some of their units close to the Thai border and these local Chinese decided to help the Malayan forces fight against them. My father told me that this was the first time that a Chinese school inspector had visited Grik after the war and he was impressed with the dedication of the teachers, and with how strongly the community supported the school.

The two trips made me realize how large Perak was. But, more than that, they gave me a sense of belonging to it that I had not felt before. Everywhere the mix of peoples was similar to what I had grown up with before leaving for China. No one thought I was foreign or strange. In fact, the only thing unusual about me was that I had studied in a university in China and circumstances had forced me to return. When people learnt that, they made clear that they were aware that China was on the cusp of historic change, and that their future home was likely to be Malaya.

One other matter impressed me. During both trips, we met people who spoke of the help they were getting from the newly formed Malayan Chinese Association. The MCA was formally established in February 1949, soon after I returned, but the event had not registered in my mind. I had thought it consisted mainly of businessmen seeking to help the government defend their interests. Because many of them were identified as Guomindang sympathizers, they were targeted as enemies by the communists. In the towns we visited, I found that MCA members were leaders of the local community and were generous supporters of the local schools. I began then to pay more attention to what the party was doing.

I particularly recall the afternoon when my father attended a Perak Chinese Chamber of Commerce reception for the MCA president, Dato' Tan Cheng Lock. It was in April 1949, two months after the MCA was formed, and communist agents threw a hand grenade at Tan Cheng Lock while he was addressing the gathering. Although badly wounded, he survived the attack. My father was lucky. His seat was near the blast but he was not hurt. That event had made my mother even more nervous about my father's travels outside of Ipoh. After our two trips south and north of Perak, I became more aware of the important role the MCA was playing in lobbying for the *jus soli* principle to be applied to everyone in the country so that more local Chinese could be given federal citizenship. The political stakes were not only about defeating the communists but also about the future of Chinese who wished to make Malaya their home. This added an extra dimension to my understanding of the difficult road ahead for the new country.

——◇✕◇——

My father had looked out for ways that I could continue my studies after I returned to Malaya, and he saw no alternative for me other than to study locally. Being in education, he knew of the British plans to merge the two colleges in Singapore into a new university. It also occurred to him that I might stand a better chance of studying there if I became a federal citizen of the new state. I was qualified to apply but it would mean giving up my Chinese citizenship. I was surprised to see how carefully he had thought this through and how willing he was for me to turn away from a China that he seemed to have mentally written off. He never explained what made him urge me to take this step and what made him act so politically, something I had never seen him do before. I could only guess that his exposure to the threats by the MNLA against his beloved Chinese schools in Perak added to his disillusionment with the corrupt Nationalist government in China, had hardened his resolve to act that way.

I was admitted to the University of Malaya before I finally received my federal citizenship, on 16th September, three weeks before I set off for Singapore. By that time, I had been preparing for the new university. I had learnt some elementary French before going to Nanjing; there, in the Department of Foreign Languages, I took German as my second foreign language. My father thought that, for a British university, it would be advantageous for me to know Latin. He found someone who could teach me Latin and encouraged me to improve my French and German. In between my teaching jobs, this kept me busy.

As it turned out, the university in Singapore assumed that in a plural society most of their students would have at least another language and did not require its students to learn a second language. So I gave up studying Latin but continued for a while to keep up my reading knowledge of French and German. Eventually, I realized that my bazaar Malay was inadequate and concentrated on the national language so that I could read its literature, not least the Generation 1945 writings coming out of Indonesia.

When I left for Singapore in October 1949, I did not foresee that I would never live in Ipoh again. I returned once for a brief stay during the summer vacation, but my father was transferred to Kuala Lumpur soon afterwards. It was many years later, in the 1960s, before I visited Ipoh and only for a day. I found that almost all my friends were working elsewhere. Walking the streets in New Town that day brought memories of how insecure and confused I was when I was growing up there because I was always preparing to go somewhere else. Ipoh had taught me that nothing was permanent, that change was always around the corner and that people could easily be cut off from their roots.

In 1949, I spent nine months reassessing my future after seeing all our family plans for China come to nothing. That led me to weigh the sense of heritage and duty that I was brought up with against the desire for my mind to be open and free. My brief encounters with an ancient civilization trying to modernize did not give me confidence in what China had become. I also realized that the slogans about race and nation that were being broadcast in Malaya had little appeal. What I knew I had was the love of my parents. They had given me my most precious possession, the urge to study. I longed to make new friends and hoped to earn trust and respect wherever I was destined to go. For that, I knew that order and harmony was best and not violence and war.

The week before I left to study in Singapore, on October 1st, 1949, Mao Zedong proclaimed the establishment of the People's Republic of China. I was happy that China had been reunified and a new China was being born, but sad that I would not be part of what would happen there. I was sure I would always be Chinese at heart and admiring of the China that my parents and my Nanjing teachers and fellow students had taught me to love. I also wanted the best for the new China that the people in China have longed for during the past half-century. I had lived nearly seventeen years in a Malay state and eighteen months in China. Yet it seemed sometimes that I cared for both in equal parts. The pull of a plural society was great, but the cultural attraction of China in all its dimensions was deep and irresistible. I was not to appreciate until much later that there was no conflict there and that the co-existence of the two had become normal for me. And then I would recall how I struggled in 1949 to adjust to the new Malaya and the new China and wonder if my life had really begun anew during that year in Ipoh.

Index

800 Heroes, The (film), 40–2, 48

Academia Sinica, 162
agrarian economy, of China, 169
air raid shelters, 111
American air and naval battles, 92
Anderson School, 32, 34, 45, 48, 85,
    95, 99, 101, 138, 189
Anti-Japanese Army, 97, 101, 203
anti-Marxist propaganda, 170
Australian National University, 175

Babai zhuangshi (film), 40
Bai, Guang, 42
baihua vernacular, 23
Baiyuzhai cihua (book of ci-poetry
    criticism), 161
Bartholomew, Freddie, 44
Beida School, 175
Beijing Foreign Languages College,
    179, 182
Bendahara, Raja, 35
Bergson, Henri, 170
Bose, Subhas Chandra, 102
British Empire, 35, 50, 165, 166, 168
    colonial power, 34

education system in, 35
Japanese invasion against, 14
military action against Malayan
    communists, 15
Opium Wars, 40
role in China's downfall, 40
British India, 34
    anti-British nationalism, 102
British Military Administration
    (BMA), 97–8, 102
Buddhist sutras, 26, 156
Burma, 14, 85, 91–2, 103

cadets-in-training, 36
calligraphy
    practice of, 38, 78, 135
    xiaokai, 7
Cambridge School Examinations,
    183–4
Cantonese language, 22, 23, 25
Carr-Saunders, Alexander, 197
    Carr-Saunders Commission, 198
Celestial Fairy Temple, 127
Central Compilation and Translation
    Bureau, 158
Ceylon (Sri Lanka), 27, 31, 34, 35, 46
Chan, Kye Choo, 75, 86

Chen, Gongbo, 141
Chen, Jizu, 75, 114
Chen, Lifu, 170
Chen, Tingzhuo, 132, 161
Cheong, Kok Ying, 101
Chiang, Ching-kuo, 144
Chiang, Kai-shek, 38–9, 137, 139,
    144, 150, 159, 162, 170
    China's Destiny, 170
Chief Inspector of Chinese Schools,
    149
China Salvation Movement, 39, 42
Chinese characters, learning of, 23
Chinese citizenship, 206
Chinese civilization, 44, 139, 167
Chinese civil war, *see* civil war
Chinese Communist Party (CCP),
    19, 39, 140, 156, 195
    fight against corruption, 203
    growth of, 203
Chinese community leaders, killing
    of, 204
Chinese currency, 68
    exchange rate with US dollar,
        143–4
    fabi notes, 143
    jinyuanjuan currency, 143–4
Chinese dialects, 27, 83, 105
Chinese Dilemma, The (2005), 82
Chinese education, 30, 33, 141
    funding to protect, 55
Chinese Eurasians, 88
Chinese identities, 82
Chinese language and literature
    courses on, 147, 155

knowledge of, 161
learning of, 88–9, 173
teachers for, 160–72
Chinese New Year festivities, 95
Chinese peasantry, plight of, 169
Chinese Peranakan (local-born), 13
    Dutch and Indonesian (Javanese)
        attitudes towards, 13
Chinese revolution (1911), 44, 47,
    139–40
Chinese schools
    development of, 12
    High School, 12–13, 20, 82, 109
    Middle School, 55
    in Perak, 39, 99
    students' morals and social habits,
        163
    support to Chinese defence
        forces, 47
Chinese society, 15, 26
Chinese university, 99, 197
Chin, Peng, 82, 204
Chongqing, 38, 65, 73, 137–8, 141,
    152, 154, 158
Chung, Sam, 90–1, 100
ci-poems, 132, 161
civil service examinations, 5
civil war, 138, 140–2, 144, 154, 163,
    186, 189, 195
classical language, 96
colonial education, 35, 96, 198
Confucian, 1–2, 6–9, 12, 24, 26, 42,
    49, 79, 84
Confucianism, 6
Confucian learning, 131

Confucian Temple district, 145, 150
Constitutional Government
    Promotion Society, 131
creative evolution, idea of, 170
cultural networks, of leading families,
    125
Cultural Revolution (1973), 101, 126,
    129, 131, 135, 156, 161, 175, 180,
    182
currency depreciation, issue of, 143–4

Daoist spirits, 127
democratic socialism, 171
Deng, Xiaoping, 101, 135, 176, 180
Department of Foreign Languages,
    14, 138, 152, 165, 206
deprivation, sense of, 94
Dewey, John, 9, 11, 79
Ding family
    ancestors of, 5
    book-based career, 6
    business skills, 6
    classical studies, 5
    Confucian values, 6
    decline of family business, 7
    destruction of, 6
    Ding Gong Guan (family home),
        7
    as extended family, 6
    family tradition, 5
    family wealth, 5–6
    foot binding custom, 7
    gathering during every meal, 5–6
    opium smoking, 6

salt business, 5
Zhenjiang, 5
Ding Gong Bridge, 8
Ding Gong Guan (Ding family
    home), 7
Ding, Quqing, 66
Ding, Yan, 3, 5
division of labour, 114
Dongtai, 5, 7, 51, 63, 132, 184
Dutch East Indies, 55–6

Elizabeth, Queen, 43
Emergency, 15, 141, 196, 203, 204
English books, caretaking for, 86–8
English fiction reading, 89, 99
English language, learning of, 46,
    59–60, 86, 90, 155
European civilization, 178

fabi notes, 143
family relations, 132–6
family's genealogy, roots of, 128–32
Fan, Cunzhong, 165
financial fiasco of August 1948, 203
Five Dynasties period, 147
food relief, for people displaced by
    war, 154
foot-binding custom, 7, 43–4
Force 136 (British Army), 97, 101
Foreign Language College, Beijing,
    158
Francis, Mrs, 31
Fujian, 21, 53, 68, 81, 153

fund-raising, for defence of China, 47–9, 69
Fu, Sinian, 162

Ginling Women's Arts & Sciences College, 150, 151
Girls Middle School, 189
government employment, 9
Great Depression, 19–20
Grik, 204–5
Guangdong, 21, 53, 68, 90, 153
Guangxi province, China, 68, 91, 133, 204–5
Guangzhou, 73, 187
guerrilla war, 171, 203
Gu, Jiegang, 166
Guo, Bingwen, 9, 11
Guomindang government (KMT), 39, 99–100, 102, 139, 141, 144, 159, 167–8, 200, 205
Guo, Moruo, 166, 174
guoyu, 21, 24, 27, 30, 80–1, 83, 90, 119
Guwen Guanzhi, 78–9

Hakka people, influence of, 68
Han dynasty, 43, 80, 89, 160
hiding, from Japanese troops
    in limestone caves, 74
    malaria attack, 74
    at timber camp, 74
higher education, 51, 142, 150, 198
Hokkien Association, 76–7, 81
Hong Kong, 37, 88, 133, 169, 195
    dollars, 143

University, 161
Hong, Xiuquan, 140
Ho, Shih-an, 23
Hou, Wailu, 156
huaqiao, 12, 55, 64, 69, 155, 161
Huaqiao Middle School, Singapore, 52, 56
Hu, Jintao, 133

imperial Confucian heritage, destruction of, 132
Imperial Salt Commission, 5
Indian National Army, 102
Indonesia, 13, 15, 82, 101–3, 207
inflation-weakened economy, 143
    as source of political instability, 163
international tribunal, findings of, 104
inter-racial revenge killings, 97
Ipoh town, 1–3, 8, 35, 58–9
    bombing of, 74
    Chinese consulate in, 188
    demography of, 27
    dominant language, 25
    economic conditions in, 91
    Education Department, 56
    fund collection, for war effort in China, 47–8
    Green Town, 27, 31, 83, 85, 86, 105–6
    Hakka people, influence of, 68
    Ipoh Security Association, 114
    Japanese garrison in, 75
    Japanese occupation of, 95, 197

map of, 28–9
memories of, 21
New Town, 24, 27, 75, 81, 90,
    118–9, 196, 207
Old Town, 27, 76, 83, 107, 197
reopening of cinemas, 99
settling at, 59

Japan
    American victory against, 92
    bombing mission, 111
    currency, 91–2, 121
    films, 89, 96
    Home Guard unit, 102
    invasion of
        China, 14
        Malaya, 14, 34, 36, 64
        Singapore, 75
        Southeast Asia, 66
    national anthem, 77
    patriotic songs, 77
    Penang, bombing of, 66
    surrender of, 93
    victory over British, 14
Japanese goods, boycott of, 41
"Japanese" (Wako) pirates, 128
Jilong (Keelung), Taiwan, 195
Jinling University, Nanjing, 133, 163
jinshi graduates, 130
jinyuanjuan currency, 143–4
journey from Surabaya to Ipoh,
    19–26
    learning Chinese characters, 23
    preparation for, 23
jus soli principle, 205–6

Kinta River, 27, 76, 77, 90
Kinta valley, 21
Korean War, 127
Kroh (Pengkalan Hulu) town, 204
Kuala Lumpur, 2, 57, 64, 81, 122,
    149, 164, 187, 189, 193, 207
Kuang, Yuchang, 193–4

land use and ownership, issue of, 169
language skills, 47, 139, 158
Lay Buddhist Home, 132
Lenggong, 204
Liang, Changling, 61
Liang, Shiqiu, 173
Li, Chun-ming, 56
Lim, Boon Keng, 12
Lin, Biao, 175
Liu, Bang, 80
Liu, Shimu, 165
Liu, Yizheng, 167
Li, Zhongqian, 62
London, 41, 44, 50, 73, 101
Longxing Temple (Hidden Dragon
    Temple), 132
Lou, Guanglai, 165
Lu, Tianshi, 179
Lu, Zhenyu, 166

Madras, 34, 107
madrasahs, 31
Majid, Abdul, 193
Malaya
    Anti-Japanese Army, 203
    British Malaya, 46
    defence of, 73

Malaya (*continued*)
    federal citizenship, 206
    guerrilla war, 171
    independence of, 171
    Japanese invasion of, 14, 34, 36,
        64, 102
        Relief Funds against, 64
    lingua franca of
        Cantonese, 95
        pasar Malay, 95
    primary schools in, 31, 33
    relation with Chinese, 188
    return to, 186
    Tanah Melayu, 103
    Women's Division, of Overseas
        Chinese, 64
Malayan Chinese Association
    (MCA), 205
    jus soli principle, 205–6
Malayan Communist Party (MCP),
    82, 97, 102, 203
    military arm of, 140
    war to liberate Malaya, 140
Malayan dollars, 143
Malayan National Liberation Army
    (MNLA), 196
    guerrilla war, 203
Malayan Peoples' Anti-Japanese
    Army (MPAJA), 97, 101–2
Malu Tianshi (film), 42
Manchu rule
    conquest of China, 43
    end of, 7
Mandarin language, 21–2, 25, 77,
    80–1, 90, 119
Mandate of Heaven, 140

Manjianghong (poem), 41
Mao, Jiaqi, 148
Mao, Zedong, 92, 207
Marco Polo Bridge, 38
Margaret, 1, 4, 128, 176
Ma Tianying, Ibrahim, 188
Maxwell School, 30–2
Mei, Guangdi, 61
"memories of fifty years", 4
Menon, K.P.S., 151
Miao, Fenglin, 166–7
Ming dynasty, 125, 128, 130, 147,
    150, 161
Ming Teh (Mingde) Primary School,
    77, 84, 95
Muda, Raja, 35

Nanhai trade, history of, 89
Nanjing, 19, 65, 193, 198
    ban against demonstrations in,
        142
    early life in, 20–1
    fall of (1927), 12, 38, 126
    getting to, 137–44
    Ginling Women's Arts &
        Sciences College, 150, 151
    Guomindang government in,
        99–100
    Higher Normal College, 9
    inflation-weakened economy, 163
    Jinling University, 133, 163
    life after Japanese rule, 138
    memories of, 21
    Nanking University, 150
    as national capital, 139, 145

Nationalist government in, 39
Taiping Heavenly Kingdom, 140
victims of the rape of, 141
Yuhuatai battles for defence of,
    151
Nanyang *huaqiao* (Overseas Chinese),
    12
Nanyang University, Singapore, 164
National Anthem, of People's
    Republic of China, 48, 167
National Central University, Nanjing,
    14, 135, 137–8, 142, 162, 184
Nationalist army, 47
    defeat of, 193
Nationalist Party, 141, 168, 206
    in Chinese civil war, 15
    loss of credibility, 143
    Northern Expedition of, 12
    in Taiwan, 195
National Southeastern University, 9
National Taiwan University, 162
Navaratnam, Mrs, 32
Nazi Germany, 74
    defeat of, 94
    invasion of Soviet Union, 74
Nelson, Horatio, 44, 50
New Fourth Army, 133, 184
Niujiazhuang village, 129
Nong Chik, Raja, 193
North-South division, 145

occupation learning, 86
opium smoking, 6, 8
Opium Wars, 40
    Opium War, The (film), 96

Outline of Chinese History, 166, 168
overseas Chinese, 168
    cause of educating, 99
    financial burden for, 69
    history of, 88
    in Hong Kong, 101
    remittances from, 54, 65
    Women's Division of, 64

Papan, town of, 111, 117
pasar (bazaar) Malay language, 25
patriotic films, 40–5
patriotic songs, singing of
    China will not die, 48
    Japanese, 77
    On the Sungari River, 48
    Volunteers Marching Song, 48
patriotism
    displays of, 39
    patriotic movement, 69
Peinan Primary School, 68, 76, 116
Peking, Treaty of, 130
Peking University, 125, 133, 175
Penang, 21, 66, 70, 95, 141, 169, 194
    bombing of, 66
People's Liberation Army (PLA),
    138, 142, 203
people's livelihood, principle of, 167,
    169, 203
People's Republic of China, 150
    diplomatic relations with
        Australia, 175
    establishment of, 207
people's rights, principle of, 167,
    169

Perak, state of, 35, 196
    Chinese schools in, 39, 99
    Perak Chinese Chamber of
        Commerce, 205
    teaching in schools in, 49
Philippines, 103, 195
post-war economy, recovery of, 196
Provincial Taizhou High School,
    128
public execution, 75–6
public speech competition, in
    English, 150

Qian, Mingshan, 177
Qian, Sezhi, 160, 173–8
Qianziwen, 78
Qianzi wen textbook, 23
Qiao, Yifan, 52, 141
Qiao, Yin-gang, 52–3
Qing dynasty, 6, 8, 125, 135, 161
    defeat by Western Powers, 131
Qingxu, 128
Qingyuan, 128
Quezon, Manuel, 104

racial tensions, 102
radio news, listening of, 99
Raffles College, 196, 198
refugee camps, 185
remittances
    Chinese government monthly
        plan for, 66
    from overseas Chinese, 54, 65

St Michael's Institution, 27, 76, 107,
    189, 190, 197

salesmen, careers as, 75
salt trade, 5
Sanguo yanyi (novel), 161
Sanjiang Gonghui, 187, 189
Sanjiang Tongxianghui, *see* Three
    Rivers (jiang) Provincial
    Association
Sanlitun village, 129
Sanmin zhuyi, 167–70
Sanzijing textbook, 24, 78
schooldays, life during, 33–4
schooling and early education, 30–6
    in language skills and other
        subjects, 46–7
    on patriotism, 47
    School Certificate subjects, 108
    school leaving class, 98, 106
    school leaving examinations, 198
semi-nomadic life, 74
Senior Cambridge Examinations, 98
Shanghai, 37, 41, 49–50, 63, 84, 133,
    137, 193
    arrival at, 62
    boarding ship to Singapore, 194
    Chinese films in, 96
    Japanese attack on, 38, 65
    Shanghai Museum, 126
Sha, Xuejun, 163
Sheldon, William H., 200
Shen, Moyu, 12
Shuihuzhuan (novel), 161
Sima Guang, 80
Singapore, 37, 47, 169
    boarding ship from Shanghai to,
        194
    defence of, 111–2

Japanese occupation of, 75
journey back to, 64
killing of Chinese in, 75
leaving of, 207
Nanyang University, 164
Naval Base, 73
travel to, 186
university in, 189, 206
Sino-Japanese films, 89
Sino-Japanese war, 14, 23, 36, 38–40,
    126, 132, 181
China's recovery after, 162
Six Dynasties, 9, 11, 156
Song dynasty, 9, 41, 166
Southern dynasties, of 5th and 6th
    centuries, 140
Southern Tang Kingdom, 146–7
Soviet communism, 167
Soviet Union
    Chiang Kai-shek's relation with,
        170
    invasion of, 74
spoken English, 60, 91
Stalin's Russia, 15
Sun, Yat-sen, 47, 88, 132, 168, 200
    appeal to Chinese in Malaya,
        168–9
    dreams for a united China, 139
    as Father of the Nation, 163
    Mausoleum, 138–9, 150
    people's rights, principle of, 169
    Three Principles of the People,
        155, 167, 171, 203
Surabaya, 12–13, 19, 22, 52, 57,
    149

Taiping Heavenly Kingdom, 5, 140,
    145
Taiping Rebellion (1851–64), 51, 130
Taiwan, 126–7, 162–3, 193, 195
Taizhou, 5, 8–9, 37, 40, 58, 62, 130,
    143
    Municipal Library, 128–9, 131
    Provincial High School, 128
Tale of Two Cities, A (film), 44, 88
Tan Cheng Lock, 205
Tangshi sanbaishou, 79
Tanjong Tualang, 74, 112, 113–14,
    115
Tao, Xingzhi, 11
Tao, Yuanming, 78
teachers, for Chinese language and
    literature, 160–72
teaching job, 68, 117, 180, 206
Three Kingdoms period, 140, 145
Three Principles of the People (book),
    155, 163, 167, 203
Three Provinces (Sanjiang), 68
Three Rivers (jiang) Provincial
    Association, 68
Tizhai jinyugao (my father's volume
    of poetry), 108
traditional China, views of, 2, 4
trip to China, 37, 61–2
    during occupation years, 105
trip, to Sun Yat-sen's mausoleum,
    138–9, 150

United Nations Relief and
    Rehabilitation Administration
    (UNRRA), 154

university education, 183
University of Malaya, 2, 162, 198
    admission to, 206
    Faculty of Arts in, 201
US dollar, exchange rate of, 143–4

volunteer corps, 36
Volunteers Marching Song, 48

Wang, Ching-wei, 38–9, 99, 140–1,
    164
    act of treachery in China, 102
    anti-Japanese activities, 103
    puppet regime of, 178
    supporters in Perak, 141
Wang clan, 4, 8–9, 130
    family biographies, 128
Wang, Dingzhu, 130, 132
Wang, Fuwen (Wang Yichu), 3, 8
Wang, Gen, 130
Wang, Gengxin, 131
Wang, Haishan, 9
Wang, Leixia, 131, 135
Wang, Shangwen, 128
Wang, Shizhen, 129
Wang, Wuchen, 129
Wang, Yinfu, 130
Wang, Yinhu, 130–1
Wang, Zhendong, 114–15
Wang, Zongyan, 9
war crime tribunals, 102
    conviction of Japanese military
        leaders, 104

war, memories of, 111–22
    air raid shelters, 111
    back in New Town, 118–19
    defence of Singapore, 111–12
    division of labour, 114
    effects of parting, 112
    end of the war, 119–22
    Japanese bombing mission, 111
    on move to Ipoh, 114–18
    rise in price of goods, 118
    shelter in the caves, 115
    stay in the jungle, 114
    Tanjong Tualang, 113–14
war movies
    cinema ticket prices, 95
    depicting American victory over
        Japanese, 93–4
    obsession with, 94
    quality of, 94
wars of independence, 15
wartime collaboration, concerns
    about, 104
wartime "education", 97
Western civilization, 44
Western imperialism, 40, 167
Widdowson, Miss, 33
Winter, Robert, 11
Women's Division, of Overseas
    Chinese, 64
World War II, 21
Wuchang uprising, 139
Wu family, 24–5
Wuhan, Choir, 47–9
Wuhan Choral Society, 69
Wu, Mi, 11

Wu, Ti Hsien, 24, 121, 189, 195
Wu, Yu-teng, 56
Wu Zetian, Empress, 43

Xiamen
    port of, 195
    Xiamen University, 12
Xiang, Yu, 79
Xiannumiao, 127
xiaokai calligraphy, 7
Xia, Zukui, 178–80, 182
Xinguowen textbook, 24
Xuanwu Lake, 150, 155
Xu, Bojiao, 126, 195
Xu, Caiming, 187
Xu, Hongbao, 125
Xu, Senyu, 125, 126
Xuzhou town, 189, 193

Yang, Chao, 156
Yang, Xianyi, 146
Yan, Yi-fu, 52, 62
Yan, Zhenqing, 9, 78
Yan, Zhongfu, 62
Yanziji massacre (1937), 151

You, Shou, 160–2, 166, 173
Yuan, Shikai, 6, 129
Yue Fei (film), 41, 44, 50
Yuhuatai battles, for defence of
    Nanjing, 151

Zeng, Zhiqiang, 60, 113
Zhang, Daqian, 126
Zhang, Ji'an, 118
Zhang, Xiong, 174–8, 182
Zhao, Xin-hou, 57
Zhengding Wangshi Jiazhuan (1893),
    131
Zhenjiang city, 5, 51, 64, 127, 132,
    177
Zhi-jia-da (ship), 53
Zhongda, 150–2, 162–3, 166, 168,
    170
Zhonghua Book Company, 187
Zhou, Enlai, 156, 175
Zhou, Fohai, 141
Zhou, Xuan, 42
zhuan calligraphy, 9, 10
Zhu, Yan, 178, 180–2
Zhu, Yuanzhang, 147, 150
Zijin (Purple) Mountain, 139